I JUST WANT YOU TO KNOW

KATE GOSSELIN

NEW YORK TIMES BESTSELLING AUTHOR

I JUST WANT YOU TO KNOW

LETTERS TO MY KIDS
ON LOVE, FAITH,
and FAMILY

ZONDERVAN®

ZONDERVAN.com/
AUTHORTRACKER
follow your favorite authors

ZONDERVAN

I Just Want You to Know
Copyright © 2010 by Katie Irene Gosselin

This title is also available as a Zondervan ebook.
Visit www.zondervan.com/ebooks.

This title is also available in a Zondervan audio edition.
Visit www.zondervan.fm.

Requests for information should be addressed to:

Zondervan, *Grand Rapids, Michigan 49530*

Library of Congress Cataloging-in-Publication Data

Gosselin, Kate.
    I just want you to know : letters to my kids on love, faith, and family / Kate Gosselin.
       p.   cm.
    ISBN 978-0-310-31896-5 (hardcover, jacketed)
    1. Twins — United States — Pennsylvania. 2. Sextuplets — United States — Pennsylvania.
  3. Multiple birth — Popular works. 4. Mother and child. I. Title.
  HQ777.35.G665 2010
  306.874'3092 — dc22   2010008387

Cover design: Michelle Lenger
Cover photography: Nigel Parry / CPi
Interior design: Christine Orejuela-Winkelman

Interior photos: Provided by the Gosselin family

Printed in the United States of America

---

10 11 12 13 14 15 16 /DCI/ 24 23 22 21 20 19 18 17 16 15 14 13 12 11 10 9 8 7 6 5 4 3 2 1

While we try to teach our children all about life,
Our children teach us what life is all about.
—Angela Schwindt

CONTENTS

DEAR KIDS

The way my kids are being raised is, without question, unconventional. Our supersized life feels normal to them right now because it's all they know, but when they grow up they may look back and wonder how things would have turned out if we had been a normal-sized family living under normal circumstances. Jon and I had always envisioned ourselves having two or three kids, but as our story turned out, we ended up with twins and sextuplets in three years. I want to share with each of my eight children about our life together so they will know without a shadow of a doubt how much I love them and how much every decision and sacrifice I made was worth it for them.

❋ ❋ ❋

I present this book to you — Cara, Madelyn, Alexis, Hannah, Aaden, Collin, Leah, and Joel — as the background on our family. You'll see how we attempted to create memories, provide for your needs, form traditions, and give you a good foundation. The time frame—from the time we moved into our house with the red door on Andrew Avenue in Elizabethtown until we moved out—holds a special place in my heart. You were all so squooshy and cuddly, and the little kids were just starting to develop their own personalities.

During these simpler times when I was at home alone taking care of all eight of you during the day, I was happy and satisfied—but I was also exhausted. Being your mommy is a big job, and one I never took lightly. And even though we didn't often venture outside the house for the first few years, I was never bored. Funny how that works.

My hope is that you see through these letters how much I love you as a group and, more important, as individuals. You each have unique qualities, characteristics, and personalities that together complete our family. Never forget that inside my hard, strict outer shell is a heart bursting with love for each of you. As I always say, I didn't set out to have eight children but I ended up with the best eight kids on the planet, and I thank God daily for each one of you.

1

ORDINARY IN AN EXTRAORDINARY WAY

We pulled into the parking lot at Friendly's restaurant for one of our rare dinners out. I got out of our Big Blue Bus and was reaching in for one of the kids when a black dog ran over and started licking my leg. Though he was obviously a fan of my leg, I wasn't a fan of the dog. I looked around and saw his owner, an older lady.

"Excuse me, could you please put him on a leash?" I asked.

"You want me to do what?"

"Could you put him on a leash? I have to get my kids out of the car and some of them are scared of dogs."

"I will not!" she said indignantly.

Another lady in a van parked nearby had watched the encounter. "What did she say?" she asked the woman with the dog.

"She told me to put him on a leash, and I said I wouldn't."

At that point, Jon and I just tried to do the best we could. We got all eight of the kids out of the bus and assembled in a line holding hands, steering clear of the dog still panting at my ankles.

"They were just on TV," the van lady said to the dog lady.

Jon and I started to lead the kids away from the bus.

"Hey, were you just on TV?" the dog lady asked. Suddenly she didn't have as much attitude.

"Yes," I said over my shoulder. I didn't want to look at her and her salivating dog. I just kept walking.

We took off across the parking lot with the woman following us. "I know who you are. I love that show!"

What do you do with that? I've had plenty of practice since that first fan encounter, but practice doesn't always make it easier. Most people are respectful. They know how to say, "Oh, how cute," and move on. My biggest concern is getting my children safely to our destination, but persistent fans want to keep the conversation going.

Some people think the show took away our privacy, and maybe our right to it; but before the show even began folks would approach us. They wanted to see the kids. Let's face it—they're cute! I get it that people are naturally drawn to their sweet little faces. I understand people's curiosity about a large family with sets of multiples and the attention it attracts in a small town. But even then I longed to be inconspicuous and do the things ordinary families did.

In those early days, people didn't approach us much; they would, for the most part, just stand back and stare. If I had paid attention, I would have seen them pointing and counting, but most of the time I didn't even notice. I was usually so hyper-focused on making sure the kids got safely to our destination that I didn't notice people's reactions unless they made it impossible for me to ignore them—like the lady with the dog. A lot of times I would say, "It's nice to meet you, but I'm sorry, I have to get my kids in the car."

The persistent fans were often more concerned about what they were getting out of me than having respect for my situation. That's probably where my perceived bad attitude toward the public started. Depending on the location, I tried to be cordial and kind, but I probably didn't always respond very well. Frankly, it bothered me that people wouldn't leave us alone. Sometimes they even wanted to touch the kids. I got very good about quickly stepping in between them before they could.

These types of encounters caused Jon and me to long for what we called a "normal" family life. For us, normal meant being able to travel outside of the house with just the ten of us—no chaperones. Normal meant my kids could get out and play freely, instead of being restrained in their strollers because we couldn't keep sixteen chubby little legs from running in eight different directions. In my fantasies about "normal," I craved a quiet life where my family and I could go out in public without people staring, pointing, and counting my kids. It was hard enough trying to be a mom of twins and sextuplets without feeling like the world was watching everything I did.

Safety is always a concern for parents of young children, but for Jon and me, any usual concern had to be multiplied by eight. For example, what if our house caught fire during the night? That was one of my greatest fears. Physically, how would two adults get eight kids out of a burning house? Every night before I went to sleep, I prayed to God to keep us safe from a fire.

When the six were infants, the best plan Jon and I could come up with was for me to get Cara and Mady. Jon would then pile the little kids into one big blanket and throw it over his shoulder like Santa as we all raced to the nearest exit. We knew that wasn't a perfect solution—the babies would roll all over each other, maybe even break a bone—but it was better than the alternative. We always kept a comforter under the cribs just in case of an emergency.

But once we were in a new house and the little kids were no longer infants, we had to come up with a new plan. Though they could walk, you can't tell six two-year-olds, "Yeah, I know it's hot and smoky, but go ahead and walk down the stairs." No, they'd be terrified. We had to come up with contingencies for every possibility. "What if the fire is at the bottom of the steps?" "What if one of them runs back upstairs to grab a comfort item?" "What if they're too scared to come to us when we call them?" Other families had fire drills; Jon and I had fire interrogations.

Another thought that kept us awake at night was who would take the kids if something happened to us. For many families, it's easy to find an aunt, grandmother, or close friend to take in a child or two.

But eight kids?

It was important to Jon and me that the kids stayed together. Who would be willing and capable of taking all of them? My brother and sister-in-law offered, but they already had four kids of their own. It would be too much to have twelve kids in one house. Their intentions were admirable, and we were grateful for the offer. But twelve kids would send even me over the edge.

We struggled to find a solution. Eventually, we named our friends as the first choice to take the kids. We chose them because their kids were older, and we felt it wouldn't be such a huge burden for them to take all eight. I trusted that they would make family visits a priority for our kids in the event that something happened to Jon and me.

House fires. Parents dying. Certainly those are extreme, unlikely events, but they are still normal concerns for most families. What wasn't normal was how complicated it was to address those concerns. We could twist ourselves in knots over the right thing to do. It was never easy. The decisions we had to make seemed harder than those made by typical families, and I longed for the simplicity of an ordinary-sized household. In my fantasies these people's lives seemed much less complicated than mine.

❊ ❊ ❊

Ordinary parents cook pancakes, but most don't quadruple the recipe. Ordinary families buy bread at the grocery store, but few of them buy it by the flat (that's twelve loaves if you're counting). Ordinary moms of two-year-olds run out of energy during the day, but I'm guessing they don't usually feel entirely depleted. From the mundane (we ate four boxes of cereal or two dozen eggs for breakfast every day) to the unusual (on Christmas we put a baby gate around our tree to protect the ornaments from the kids and the kids from the ornaments) our normal was never ordinary.

Our culture just isn't set up for supersized families.

Take trash for example. No one ever thinks about their trash. They collect it from their house once or twice a week, set it by the curb, and forget it until the next week. Not us. We lived in an area where there were strict limits on the number of bags you could throw away each week, and we always exceeded those limits—especially when the kids were in diapers. We easily had two bags of trash on an ordinary day, more on birthdays and holidays. By the end of an average week, we'd have four huge cans filled with bags of garbage and diapers.

I remember so many Sundays nights when Jon would be in the garage rationing out what garbage he could put out and what he could hold back for the next week. It was like a game of schoolyard trading where we always got the bad deal. "I'll trade one bag of dirty diapers for two bags of kitchen refuse that maybe I can compress down into a single bag to put out next week." But each week, the same problem only got worse.

One solution was to call our neighbor and friend, Miss Beverly. She came over weekly to fold our laundry and was always willing to help us out. She and her husband never used all of their garbage allotment, so Sunday nights Jon would wheel a trash can down a few streets and up a hill to leave it at her house.

I know it seems crazy to worry about trash, but Jon and I spent a lot of time in those days thinking about it. We would fantasize about normal family-sized trash the way other people dream of white picket fences.

During that time, we exceeded our trash quota so often that we left presents on top of the trash cans in hopes the sanitation workers would take everything we put out. Sometimes we left little snacks, baked goods, or candy — anything we had.

But not every problem could be solved logistically; sometimes we just had to make do. For example, some parents worry about their kids watching too much TV; I worried that my kids couldn't see the TV. We moved an old TV into the babies' room so they could watch a movie before their nap. But because the TV was small, and the perimeter of the room was filled with cribs, there wasn't a central location that gave all of the kids a good view of the screen. Several of the kids, Hannah, Leah, and Alexis, especially, couldn't see it too well. But we had to make do. Again, this was an issue I was sure normal families never faced — but it was another small thing that added to the guilt I felt.

Trash logistics and six little faces trying to view a TV screen aren't life-shattering issues. But in our family, the most ordinary activities could feel extraordinary. That also meant that unexpected events, like a sick kid, could feel downright harrowing.

❊ ❊ ❊

Sickness is serious business at our house. Colds and flu don't just travel through our family; they take up residence in each and every child. But sometimes it's not just the illness that brings us down. The ancillary things like doctor's visits, prescription refills, and health professionals who don't understand our needs further complicate daily life.

Lots of families with kids have stories about how all the kids got sick at once. As a nurse, that part isn't hard. I'm used to taking care of multiple patients at the same time. For me, the hardest part is trying to get each and every child to the doctor's office when (and only when) they need to be seen.

In December 2006, five of the six had been coughing for nearly a week. I'm not the kind of mom who runs her child to the doctor for every little sniffle, but their coughs had gone on for a long time and I was particularly worried about Leah. When I put her into her high chair one day, I thought I heard her wheezing. I decided to lis-

ten to her chest with my stethoscope, and when I did, I heard crackling and more wheezing.

I called the doctor's office and asked if Leah could be seen that day.

"Well, we don't really have any appointments available today."

"Can you just fit me in between appointments?"

"We don't usually do it that way."

"I know," I said, "but I'm a nurse and I've lis-

Big sister Mady lovingly helping Leah with her breathing treatment.

tened to her chest and it doesn't sound good. I think she should be seen by a doctor. I'll take whatever you've got; I just need my child to get in today." Finally, the assistant gave me an appointment and I hung up. Now I had to find a babysitter to stay with the rest of the kids.

Most moms know how hard it is to be seen by a doctor at the last minute. Imagine trying to coordinate the one appointment available in your physician's schedule with the schedule of a babysitter to watch your other seven kids. Taking them with me wasn't an option. I called everyone I could think of and no one was available. As it grew closer to the appointment time I only had one option left—call Jon home from work early. I hated to do that unless it was a real emergency.

Jon came home to stay with the kids, and I was a little late for the appointment, but I was so glad I followed my instinct. My tiny girl had pneumonia! Poor Leah! I was right to insist that she be seen. Had I waited a day, who knows how sick she might have become? The doctor had me start her on a nebulizer, and she prescribed an antibiotic—Zithromax.

I picked up the prescription on the way home and gave her the first dose shortly after we got back. Unfortunately, my poor baby threw up fifteen minutes later. She was hysterical. I was afraid she had thrown up the medicine and I wasn't sure whether or not to give her another dose. She needed to be on it, but I didn't want her to overdose, and it was too late to call the pediatrician by then. Day one of the illness was anything but smooth.

The next morning Aaden seemed to be doing worse so I listened to his lungs. They also sounded crackly. I called the pediatrician, but before they would put me through to the nurse, the front office staff wanted to know what I needed.

"Well, now Aaden's lungs sound crackly … Yes, I had Leah in there yesterday and her lungs sounded the same way … She has pneumonia. So I was wondering if the doctor could call in a prescription of Zithromax for Aaden too? Okay, I'll talk to the nurse …"

When the nurse called back, I repeated all of the information and answered her questions too. But then the conversation got weird.

"The doctor would never do something like that!" she said suddenly.

"Like what?" I asked.

"Call in a prescription for a patient she hasn't seen."

To get my kids the medical care they needed, I had to work hard to convince the office staff that when one of my kids got sick, the others did too. Finding a last-minute babysitter for seven so I could take one sick child to the pediatrician was part of my job as a mom of eight little kids. And repeatedly calling the doctor for appointments, prescriptions, and refills had to be done no matter how much I annoyed the office staff.

I was quickly learning that we weren't normal by the world's standards, but I also found out that with enough persistence, we could make things work. In the end, Aaden was seen by the pediatrician and was also treated for pneumonia. I've learned to always trust my mommy instincts.

If I learned anything during our time in Elizabethtown, it was that our dreams of "normal" as defined by an average-sized family weren't possible. Our logistics and our way of doing things was never normal and never would be, but we learned to stop comparing ourselves to other families, and we redefined what normal meant to us.

Normal for us meant, in part, having mounds of trash and weeks of illness; but it also meant having large group fun we could never have had with a smaller family, like team sports and playing school.

Another difference in our family was that we put extra effort into giving the kids special, individual opportunities. We knew they didn't get much time alone, so being intentional about allowing them space and attention was more important for us than for other families.

Redefining normal helped us to accept that things for us would be different, and whether it was good or bad depended on what we made of each situation.

I think every family needs to understand what makes their household work—even if it doesn't function quite like other families. During our time in that house, we learned to make a new kind of ordinary, a Gosselin normal that worked for Jon and me and for our kids. We learned we could feel like a regular family when we went out and made it home safely without any major logistical issues. (When that happened Jon and I would high-five each other because we felt so, well, normal.)

We stopped comparing ourselves to other families and set about making our own path in the world. People still stared at us and counted us when we went out. Our safety and health issues were still magnified times eight. We still ate more boxes of cereal and more eggs at breakfast than other families did. But we began to see all of that as our normal.

Learning to redefine our expectations was a huge blessing because it was during those years that our show really took off. By the time we left Elizabethtown, we would once again have to redefine a new normal, one that included even more stares and pointing, as well as lights, cameras, and a whole lot of action.

Letter to Cara

Dear Cara,

I waited my whole life to be your mommy. You are what I dreamed of when I thought of being a mother. Although I knew I'd love you a lot, I had no idea the depth of my love for you ... until you were in my arms!

My love for you is a lot more than hugs and kisses, snuggles and cuddles—although those things are extremely important and irreplaceable. However, the things you don't notice so much—the decisions I make that affect your life now and in the future, the ways I keep you safe and protect you, the life skills I teach you—these things also greatly impact and make up a mommy's love.

My first few years as a mommy, taking care of you and Mady, were absolutely some of the best years of my life. At times, being a mom was the most difficult task I had ever embarked on; however, I was always aware of the blessing that you and Mady were to me. I felt honored and privileged to be your mommy. Two gifts given to me, when I felt undeserving of even one!

I never said it out loud, but when I was pregnant with you, I deeply hoped and prayed for two baby girls. And on that day in May 2000 when I had my ultrasound, I found out my dream of "two pinks" had come true! I hurried home and began preparing your pink and purple pastel nursery. And of course I couldn't resist buying any and every pink and purple coordinating outfit available.

My feelings of maternal bliss soared, and I spent every moment imagining what it would be like to be a mommy. Even though my pregnancy was difficult—I was sick most of the time—I kept myself focused on the delivery day when I would see your precious little face for the first time.

On your birthday, October 8, 2000, when I went into labor and Daddy took me to the hospital, I was very excited but very afraid. Just as you were about to be born, I thought to myself, "There are two of us and very soon we will be three!" (Adding Mady six minutes later made us four!)

When I saw your little face for the first time, I cried at the miracle of birth. I was officially a mommy—your mommy! I brought you home and didn't know who you were. I learned quickly that you were gentle, kind, and sweet. You were a patient baby and child.

In the first few days, I noticed a little red mark on the left side of the bridge of your little nose. Every day it became more distinct and apparent. Finally, I realized it was a birthmark, and later our pediatrician confirmed that it was a hemangioma. I felt sure I had caused the birthmark and was very upset (which was the very beginning of my now infamous mommy guilt). To me, you were perfect, birthmark and all. You were a beautiful little girl who was perfectly healthy—and for that I was grateful!

One day, when you were about three, you were playing outside in the driveway and a little girl walking by with her grandfather stopped to play. She asked about your hemangioma on the side of your nose, and Mady stepped in with the details as to why you had the "strawberry." She said an angel with red lipstick kissed you before you left heaven. That's what I had told you when you asked about it.

You were a sweet and quiet little girl. You often said "Mm hmm" when asked a question, and you smiled like a little angel. You usually let Mady do the talking for you, and she did a wonderful job. You have been a joy to raise, and you have taught me that my love as a mommy is endless.

Over the years, as you have grown into a bright and beautiful young lady, I have watched you change, but I have never lost sight of my goals as your mommy. My choices and decisions then and now have remained constant: I want the best out of life for you. My children are my most precious belongings, and I take seriously the responsibility God gave me when he entrusted you to me. Although our family life has changed a lot over the years, my love for you will never change. I will always love you the same—and more—than I did the first time my arms wrapped around you.

I have appreciated the help you have given me—especially over the last year as I have had to care for you and your brothers and sisters more and more as a single parent. I am amazed at your ability to know that I need your help more and at your cheerful willingness to give of yourself. Serving dinner plates, emptying the dishwasher, and overseeing cleanup are just a few examples of this help. Everyone pitching in, I believe, is the foundation of our bond as a family. You make me so proud!

I am an open book to you, Cara. I have done and will do my very best to guide you and help you navigate the sometimes tricky paths in life. I will help you by sharing my personal life experiences. Life is always difficult, but it is how you choose to perceive it and handle the difficulties that matters most. Never compromise what you firmly believe in. Resist the urge to take the easy road. The difficult road—the one of honor, perseverance, and honesty—is most rewarding.

My prayer for you is that you will develop a deep love for God. I pray that firm convictions will define you, and that you will always take an uncompromising stand for what you believe. I dream for you a happy and fulfilling life, career, and family. I'll be there, Cara, in whatever capacity is most helpful to you.

Love forever and always, no matter what,

Mommy

2

SCHEDULING TODDLERS

As far as space goes, the move to our Elizabethtown house was long overdue. For quite some time we had been bursting at the seams in our Dauphin Avenue house, so this move was not only logistically and financially smart (Jon's commute would decrease from ninety minutes to twenty minutes), it was going to give us the space we needed in order to breathe easier.

Once in our new house, however, we took note of the many pitfalls and dangers the house contained. One example was the huge flight of stairs that led to the kids' rooms. After I visualized trying to catch six toddlers tumbling down the stairs at once, we realized that our first task in this new house was to teach the little kids how to safely go up and down the stairs. So we began what we called stair lessons. "First, sit on your heinies," I said, demonstrating, "with your feet out in front like this. Then keep your hands next to you and slowly slide down one step at a time."

Even though this seemed like the safest method, I was still afraid of a domino effect. If one kid tripped or slipped on the stairs, he could literally take out everybody else. So during the lessons, I would stand halfway in the middle of the stairs, filled with fear that this could be really bad, and do my best to guide all six of them, twenty-two-month-olds sitting on their cushy diapers and bumping down the steps.

Aaden, Alexis, Joel, and Collin climbing the stairs. We climbed up and "bumped" down.

❋ ❋ ❋

Navigating steps was at the top of the list of things to do, but organizing the basement playroom was important too. Cleanup, as every parent knows, is extremely frustrating. Everybody makes the mess, nobody owns the mess, and nobody wants to clean up the mess. Every single day. Two or three times a day. And with my myriad of children, I wanted to make cleanup as easy as possible. Even though the little kids were only two, I knew they could help with this task.

We put up huge open shelving along an entire wall in the basement. I took pictures of what belonged in each basket and hung photos on the front of the containers, so everyone knew what belonged where and could help ... or so I hoped.

❋ ❋ ❋

With eight young kids, we generated more laundry than you can imagine, so we needed to install our own Laundromat of sorts. The original laundry room had a closet with accordion doors. We removed them, put up shelving and racks for drying clothes, and installed a utility sink. Most important, we had two sets of washers and dryers. When the front loading washers were first installed, they provided hours of entertainment. The kids watched in amazement as their clothes spun around and around.

Because the room led to the back deck, we also used it as a mudroom. When the kids got dirty playing outside, we could bring them into the laundry room to remove their muddy clothes, clean them up in the sink, and send them upstairs to take a bath. I could easily sweep the sticks, mud, leaves, garbage, and whatever else they tracked in, right back outside. (Yes, I did allow them to play in the mud.)

All-day entertainment! The little kids watch as their clothing is washed in our new washing machines.

❀ ❀ ❀

Stair lessons. Basement organization. Our own Laundromat. Moving in, we made this house work for us. And though it was a simple time, it was very fulfilling for us. We were busy, but because we stuck to our schedules, Jon and I worked well together as a team. With eight kids, we had to learn what worked best for us, but we were handling everything together.

During the first year of the little kids' lives, before we moved to Elizabethtown, many volunteers helped us. But now Jon and I were settling into doing most everything ourselves. Nana Janet continued to show up faithfully every week to play with the kids and to do our ironing. Miss Beverly also came weekly to fold our laundry. Other family members and friends stopped by, and I took any assistance I could get. While I appreciated getting a few things done without interruption, the kids always enjoyed seeing someone different. But for the most part, we were independent.

Routine is what made our independence possible. Every day was pretty much the same. We did everything over and over again. The only variations in the schedule were what I was making for dinner and what phone calls I had to make — unless somebody got sick and threw a monkey wrench into the day. This routine, logistically speaking, meant I never sat down unless I was folding laundry or sleeping.

That first year in the Elizabethtown house with our young family holds some of my best memories. At that time, life seemed challenging, stressful, and exhausting; but looking back, it was manageable and satisfying to know we could do it all by ourselves.

❀ ❀ ❀

Our daily routine would start around seven or seven-thirty in the morning. I would head upstairs to get the little kids who were waiting in their rooms for me to change their diapers and dress them.

I'd hang a grocery bag on the knob of the dresser and fill it to the top with their diapers.

One day as I was changing Alexis, I looked into her beautiful brown eyes.

"I kinky [stinky]."

"Yes, Sassy, you sure are."

Playing in the nursery. Note: Even an alcove was used for a crib!

I finished changing her and moved on to Joel. After everyone had a clean diaper, which took about half an hour, I threw the bag down the stairs. Hannah bumped down and then took the bag to the kitchen, declaring, "My diapies."

I followed her, opening the kitchen door. "Hurry."

"Fies [flies]," she said as she hurled the bag into the garage, kicking the bag as was often necessary. We slapped five. "Thanks, Hanni."

I used to tell her to hurry when throwing the trash out since there were flies that would come in, and so this interaction just became part of our schedule every day.

Leah tried to get in on this ritual, but she gave up trying to compete with Hannah and came up with her own job. She would ask to turn off the "lie" [light]. Since she couldn't actually do it, she just pretended by sticking her hand near the switch while I turned it off. They each liked to find their own rituals and tasks around the house, and I enjoyed watching them discover their independence.

After diaper changes and clothes, the next task for the day was the first round of meals: make breakfast, feed breakfast, clean up breakfast, which was always right before make lunch, feed lunch, clean up lunch, and then followed by make dinner, feed dinner, clean up dinner. The endless cycle.

For breakfast, I often made a big bowl of oatmeal with organic quick oats, which was easy, fast, healthy, and inexpensive—plus the kids loved it. I would add blueberries or strawberries or brown sugar and cinnamon, or whatever we had on hand to make it different.

In the summer, after breakfast we would be outside until lunch, many times having a picnic lunch. We loved warm weather! The kids would run around outside, and after eating lunch, with a flip of the blanket, cleanup was done. In the summer, we also loved going to

We visited a local farm to see their newborn baby goats.

Henry and Linda's, an Amish couple with five young boys. They grew organic produce—unofficially organic, they just didn't spray. They grew everything under the sun! We would get strawberries and vegetables and all kinds of produce, which would then determine what we were having for dinner that night.

The kids loved going for a drive to Henry's, even if they didn't get out of the van. And if we didn't make it there in the mornings, and if someone was babysitting the kids at home, I'd run over there while doing my errands; or I'd go when Jon got home from work. Sometimes I'd go to Henry's twice a day as he would call me to take his leftover produce very inexpensively. Whatever I didn't use, I'd give away to family, friends, or neighbors.

I loved cooking with the fresh produce, and my challenge, especially if I had extra from the end of the day, was to figure out what to come up with from the ingredients. I would sometimes chop peppers and freeze them for stir-fry. I froze sixty quarts of strawberries one year. I learned to shred zucchini and freeze it to make zucchini bread in the winter. I also learned from Linda that I could freeze corn on the cob unshucked and make it in the winter as a treat. I felt really good about serving my family picked-from-the-garden-that-morning produce, and the kids loved to say, "Jesus made it, Henry grew it, Mommy cooked it, and we ate it!"

Having picnics and fresh produce was great in the summer, but such activities were much harder to do in the winter—and eight young kids always had plenty of energy to burn. We tried to do crafts often, but one winter morning we were all bored, so I started brainstorming possible things we could do. I had started to change my thinking from being a mom to being a preschool/daycare organizer when it came to projects and activities we could do during the day. I would often research online to find something that would work within our constraints: things that were inexpensive, done with one or two adults supervising, and had manageable cleanup. Not an easy task, but doable with a shift in thinking.

I had heard of using shaving cream as an activity and had actually stocked up with a few cans the week before. I used this monotonous winter morning as an excuse to test out the project. I sat all the kids at the table and gave them each a pile of shaving cream. "Swirl it around, mold it in your hands, draw shapes with your fingers, just don't put it in your mouth." These were my only instructions.

Hannah having fun with shaving cream!

The kids loved it! They played happily for a long time, moving the white foam around on the table with their hands, and the cleanup was easy. In fact, my kitchen table looked great, like I had just conditioned it with special cleaner.

Then I heard from Mady the words that made my day: "Mommy, you're the best mom ever!"

Really, shaving cream? If only every day were this easy...

Other craft activities we did, especially in the cold winter months, included drawing with crayons, paper plate art, puppets, and Play-Doh — edible and nonedible varieties, which I made in large batches.

The back of our kitchen cabinets faced our dining room, so we displayed our newest art for all to see. Whenever we finished a project, I would write down their names as well as the title of the art, which was always something random: Hannah's "dat," Collin's "line," Aaden's "mess," Leah's "garden," etc. Then we would swap out the old pictures with the new.

Leah with her Magna Doodle art. I wanted to remember these creations before the kids erased them.

I tried not to use glue and markers or anything else that could get out of control easily. It wasn't that I was afraid of messes per se, which wasn't altogether untrue at that time; it was that each kid still needed help with glue and scissors. With just me helping each one, the other kids could quickly have a meltdown waiting a half hour for their turn. I had learned to try to avoid situations that resulted in meltdowns if at all possible. One of my favorite activities at this time included stickers. Mrs. Grossman's Stickers, a California-based sticker company, had sent us tons of stickers, which we used frequently. They were cute, the kids loved them, and they were easy to control for messes.

I would say, "Stickers go on …?"

And the kids would respond, "People or paper."

❁ ❁ ❁

After lunch, no matter what season, we had blessed naptime. This was my chance to get things done, to clean up from the morning, start laundry, and start dinner.

Since cooking is my way to relieve stress, starting dinner was often my favorite time of day. With the little kids sleeping, I could zone out, thinking only of my dinner creation. I loved using organic and healthy ingredients that I found at Henry's or on sale and turning them into a meal.

Whenever I found a good deal, I would either nab as much as I could or ask someone else to pick up extra for me. I remember one day when my sister Kendra came to our house with 225 cans of tomatoes—organic tomatoes, that is—to add to the 25 cans I had already picked up myself from Sharp Shopper, a discount store near her house. She also brought 20 pounds of organic butter. I was thanking God with great enthusiasm that day. The tomatoes were only 79 cents each, which was half of what they cost on sale at Giant. Such great buys!

One day we found strawberries at Sam's Club for $1.50 a pound—

organic, of course. I sent Jon back the next day for three more flats. Even we wouldn't eat all that, but I knew I could freeze them. I constantly prayed that we would have enough to satisfy our needs, and God kept providing.

Grocery shopping was a big deal. When I was planning ahead and cooking in bulk, I would write out an ingredient list for about fifteen recipes and compile it into a grocery list. The list would practically be a book, and the amount of food it represented was shocking: 13½ pounds ground beef, 5 pounds chicken, 1 pork roast, and so many other things. I often cooked a plethora of meals and froze them to pull out and use on a day gone awry. This is where planning ahead could literally save the day. I learned early on that there is no way to create a meal for ten on a moment's notice.

Our shoe angel Connie sent us hooded towels one Christmas and the kids posed in them for her.

After dinner during the summer months, Jon and I would take everyone outside to play until dark. In the winter, we would head downstairs for family time. Jon and I were beyond exhausted by that time of the day, but we loved being in the same room together with the kids toddling around. This was when we'd clean up the toy explosion in the basement playroom and try to teach the little kids how to match the toys to the pictures on each basket. Then Jon would lie on one sofa and I would lie on the other, just trying to get a bit of rest before our last big task for the night: bath time.

Soon everyone toddled up the stairs for bath and bedtime. That was Jon's time with the kids, and he was so thorough and involved—and fast! He quickly earned the title of Bath Man. He would bathe the kids every night and put them to bed every night. During that time, I would start working on whatever I didn't get to finish that day—cleaning the kitchen, grocery shopping, laundry, etc. It wasn't unheard of for me to be doing my eighth load of laundry after ten p.m. I tried not to get behind, but if even one kid was sick, it threw off our entire schedule. We could go from eight loads to sixteen in no time flat!

At the kitchen table for a yummy meal.

❈ ❈ ❈

Even on the weekends, we had to follow our strict schedule. After all, everyone still had to eat and sleep and clean and play.

My favorite Saturday breakfast was pancakes ("cancakes," as Aaden calls them), which I loved to make. After I stopped working, Saturday also meant my least favorite thing: cleaning day! I remember one Saturday when Jon helped me clean the upstairs, the kids' rooms, and then took all the kids outside in the beautiful sunny 70 degree weather. I finished up the cleaning and then fed everyone lunch outside so we wouldn't have to clean the dining room again (the chore that we both dread the most). In the afternoon, Jon ran errands and I cleaned the bathrooms downstairs and the floors.

Once a season I would go through all of the kids' clothes to set aside things we needed to give away (often to another family with multiples) and replace with clothing that was given to us—mostly from my best friend, Jamie, who had twin girls a year younger than Cara and Mady and a son one year older than the little kids. I would store the clothes in labeled bins in the attic—more than enough for my six to wear. The trick was making sure I had the right sizes available since they wore a few different sizes at any one time. When Cara was between a five and six, Mady was not quite a five yet in length. We didn't have room in the drawers to keep any sizes not currently needed, so the sorting process had to be accurate.

The endless hair designs on Sunday mornings before church—
one of our carefully scheduled tasks.

Sunday mornings we left the house at 8:30 to attend church at 9:30, which meant I needed to be up by 6:30, lay out the kids' clothing, and start getting ready. When everyone woke up, Jon started dressing them while I was getting ready. When I was done, Jon started getting ready, while I did the girls' hair, packed the comfort items and food, which included breakfast, juice cups, a bottle of juice for refills (one bottle was only one cup per child), and snacks for on the way home from church. When we were finished loading everything and everyone into the car and started driving away, I would check the clock, which strangely always read 8:38 a.m. We were scheduled to the minute at times, but we had to be.

Schedules and routines were so important for us to survive, so we didn't get lost in details. Time of breakfast, bedtime, everything was predictable. We had to remove the guesswork in order to survive. Being late for a meal could set off a chain reaction of starving kids having meltdowns and chaos erupting.

Letter to Madelyn

Dear Madelyn,

Because of you, I am a mommy! I waited my whole life to be your mommy. As a little girl, I dreamed of the day that I would hold you, my baby, in my arms.

I had two sets of twin dolls when I was young. I got Abigail and Artie (you know them well; you all play with them!) when I was three years old. Abigail is made of fuzzy pink fabric and she has a plastic head; Artie—named after your great grandpa, Arthur—is the same, but the fuzzy material is blue. I also had Gina and Geoffrey that Grandma made for me. They were a little bit like Cabbage Patch Kids, with bald plastic heads. They were well made—though a little bit scary looking (sorry, Grandma!)—and I loved them a lot and spent many hours feeding and dressing them.

I'll never forget the day I had my first ultrasound and the doctor saw a little circle that was Cara, and then he found an even smaller circle—little you! I was so extremely happy to be having twins! I had dreamed of being a mommy of twins since I cared for Abigail and Artie and Gina and Geoffrey.

On your birthday, October 8, 2000, Daddy took me to the hospital five weeks before your due date, but I had spent a month on bed rest at home, and you were expected a little bit early anyway. Cara was born first, as you know, and you came six minutes later at 5:47 p.m. I remember that you had a short cord. You were closely connected to me! And your first cry was loud and low-pitched. I caught my first glimpse of you when you were being warmed and assessed—so beautiful and precious! You were a little smaller than Cara and more Asian in appearance, more like Daddy.

I was so excited to bring you and Cara home and to start caring for you. Everything in our green and white house—where your nursery was wall-to-wall pink and purple—was awaiting your arrival. I know you remember that house, Mady. We just talked about it together yesterday. It was a duplex home that we shared with Uncle Tom and Aunt Jen, who lived right next door. It had a tiny backyard where we played the following spring when you and Cara could sit alone. Daddy hung infant swings from the small back porch overhang. You spent many hours in those swings!

Those were very busy, but some of the best times. Life felt manageable and enjoyable to me then. I thoroughly enjoyed waking up every morning and planning your meals, schedule, and outfits.

As a baby, you were particular. Your Poppy called you "fickle." And he was right. You made your requests known even before you had words to explain them.

One time, when you were eleven months old, I took just you to the grocery store. To keep you occupied while I was shopping, I handed you a small plastic cell phone toy that was hanging in the aisle between the cereal boxes. When you reached out to take it from me, you said, "Thanks."

I said in total shock, "Mady, did you just say thanks?"

You said, "Mm hmm."

I said louder and more surprised, "Mady, did you just answer me?"

And again you said, "Mm hmm."

This blew me away and I am sure everyone shopping in that store knew it! That was my first conversation with you, Mady. You weren't even a year old yet. You were clever from the beginning, and well spoken. You have grown and changed from that tiny particular baby into an intelligent and beautiful young lady.

Being the best mommy I can be for you has always been my goal. I have always wanted the best out of life for you. Our family has changed, and that has been difficult for all of us. I assure you that all of the decisions I have made as your mommy are best for you, although they may not always appear that way now. Someday when you are older, I hope that it will be clearer for you to see; and I will always be ready to talk to you about it. Please know that even though there has been a lot of change in our family, my love for you will never change.

I have been doing my best to support you and help you through our rough times, but I have also appreciated the support you have shown me. You stepped up and contributed: Giving out vitamins, loading the dishwasher, helping to stock the juice cabinet — just to name a few examples. These are all things I have greatly appreciated. I have really come to rely on you and Cara, and you both make me so proud.

I want you to work hard and always do your best in everything, Mady. I am committed to being by your side, teaching you the important principals in life — things like integrity, which is moral soundness, trustworthiness, goodness, and honesty. These qualities will carry you far in life if you will strive to embody them.

Honesty especially sticks out to me. You and I were just discussing this quality the other day when you chose to lie about the beach towel on the laundry room floor! My repetitive words to you and your brothers and sisters, "Always tell the truth," are imperative. Develop a reputation of truth. Work hard through life and don't let the easy path lure you. The difficult path is the most rewarding path and the one that will bring the most satisfaction.

You have heard me say many times to always do your best. That doesn't always have to mean the best—as in always placing first—but make it your best! I desire for you a fulfilling life, Mady. I pray that you grow up to love God deeply and allow him to guide your choices. I hope for you a satisfying career, family, and life as a whole.

I'll be here, Madelyn Kate Rene (the additional middle name added by me and well loved by you!) for you every single step of your way to help you any way I can. If I become annoying someday, just let me know. I just want you to know how very loved you are.

Love forever and always, no matter what,

Mommy

3

BABY STEPS

When our fans think about our travels as a family, they think of the big trips they saw on television — renewing our vows in Hawaii, skiing in Utah, or spending time at the beach in North Carolina. But in those early days, "traveling" to us meant leaving our driveway. And we didn't do that often. Until the sextuplets were thirteen months old, we didn't even own a vehicle we could all fit in. People had given us money over the years, and we spent sparingly and saved what we could because we weren't sure how long our unemployment would last. But once Jon was securely back to work, we used some of that savings to put a down payment on the Big Blue Bus. That bus was the difference between going nowhere and going anywhere we wanted.

After we moved to Elizabethtown, we didn't stay home all the time. Maybe it was because things finally felt under control — we had a schedule and things were running smoothly. Maybe it was

The Big Blue Bus! What a giant lifesaver.

because the kids were a little older and more mobile. But more than anything, I think it was because we missed our church. When we lived on Dauphin Avenue in Wyomissing, our church was only a few miles away; but from Elizabethtown, it was almost fifty. Moving to the new house was necessary because it was so much closer to Jon's work, but we felt isolated and alone. We wanted to go back to our church.

For many parents, getting themselves and their kids up, dressed, and out the door for church on Sunday is a spiritual hurdle. For us, it was the biggest logistical challenge we had ever undertaken. When Jon and I started talking about going back to our church, we weren't sure it was something we could pull off. But we wanted to try.

On the first Sunday, we got the kids up, fed them breakfast, and loaded them into the car. By the time we pulled out of the driveway, we knew we were going to be late. The service started at 9:30, so that meant we had to leave no later than 8:30 to allow time to get there, get the kids unloaded, and get everyone in their proper places. Being late meant we were a little stressed by the time we sat down for the service. But other than the timing that first week, things went smoothly and the kids did well. On the drive home, we discussed what we could do differently the following week.

When the kids were that little, much of our time together was spent thinking about logistics, planning, or implementing plans, because nothing was easy. Jon and I would work through the details of an upcoming outing together. To me it was a challenge and I took pride in it. If something didn't work, I'd think it through until I came up with a workable solution.

The next Sunday, we made a few adjustments to our schedule. But we still ran late. "There has to be a way to make this work, Jon."

"This is a crazy idea ..." he said, pausing as he merged into traffic. "But what if they ate breakfast in the car?"

"What could the kids eat that wouldn't be messy?"

We reviewed several options, but they all ended with food on the floor mats or eighty sticky fingers needing to be cleaned.

Then I had an idea: "Dry cereal! They'd have their juice cups to drink from, and if we could somehow attach the cereal to their seats, they could eat it with one hand."

Easter purses that became breakfast pouches.

"Let's try it."

My inspiration came later that week while doing laundry. Hanging up the girls' Easter dresses, I remembered each dress came with a matching drawstring purse. What if I put a sandwich bag packed with cereal inside each pouch and attached it to their car seats? Between the big and little girls' dresses, and an extra dress we ended up with somehow, we had six pouches. The pouches had pink polka dots and stripes, but I didn't care. They'd work just fine.

That Sunday, Jon and I secured the kids in their car seats and looped the drawstrings through their buckles. Each got a juice cup, and for the next hour they happily ate their breakfast. This was a logistical breakthrough! From then on, we were never late to church. It may seem like a small victory to some, but to us it was huge. It gave us the confidence we needed to attempt other kinds of travel. Our dry cereal solution convinced us that with enough forethought and preparation we could successfully navigate the outside world.

Oh, how wrong we were. No matter how hard Jon and I worked to master logistics for different situations, it turned out there were some things that even we couldn't plan for.

For Memorial Day 2006, Jon and I wanted to do something special with the kids. We had mastered our weekly visit to church; it was time to take another step. Finances were still an issue. Whatever we did had to be free because we didn't have extra money. We decided on the zoo, but not just any zoo. We wanted to go to the National Zoo in Washington, DC. In typical Gosselin style, we didn't step out of our comfort zone—we plunged.

This would be our first road trip in the Big Blue Bus and we had a couple of things to deal with first. The first was the lack of rear air-conditioning—a $4,000 option we couldn't afford. We bought clip-on fans and did whatever we could to make it cool enough to drive, but on really hot afternoons it wasn't safe for the kids.

Second, while we had unlimited options for customizing a van like ours, we couldn't afford any of them. To make the bus work for us, we learned to customize it ourselves. For example, the bus didn't have a front console so I found a cooler with a pop-up tray and cup holders. That made it easier to store and serve the juice I always brought with us. Juice boxes were expensive so I used juice from bottles and diluted it.

I found plastic drawers that fit under the van seats and stocked them with essentials like diapers and wipes. But I also included other supplies like disposable bibs, trash bags, Band-Aids, paper towels, blankets, and an extra outfit for each kid. Whatever we could possibly need, it was there and neatly organized. For a while, I even put in a pack of swimmies in case we ended up at a friend's house to swim.

We customized that van in ways that it was never meant to be customized, but I wanted to make sure we always had what we needed. I took great pride in restocking the bus. Because the van was so well supplied, even if I forgot something, chances were that I could make do with what I had. And having what we needed was the difference between a miserable trip and a wonderful trip. It's also why a long car ride didn't scare me. We were prepared.

Jon even researched the zoo's terrain. When he learned there were hills, we decided to take our six-seat stroller with big wheels instead of our two three-seat strollers with very small wheels. Since the kids sat two-by-two with each row higher than the one before it, this would give each child an unobstructed view of the animals.

On the big day, I packed breakfast, lunch, and extra snacks. When traveling, food does wonders for our kids! Jon loaded the van and checked the weather. It was supposed to be overcast with no precipitation.

"It's not supposed to rain, right?" I asked.

"Nope, it's not supposed to rain," said Jon as he removed the front wheel of the stroller so he could fit it into the back of the bus.

The last thing we packed before leaving was the comfort bag. Each child used a different stuffed animal or blanket to help them fall asleep. Alexis had her pink blankie. Leah and Aaden had their chewies—burp cloths they had become attached to. Joel had a stuffed dog with a colorful sweater that he named Doggy Man. Collin had Ducky or Bear ("Bay-uh"), a stuffed animal/blanket combination, and Hannah had one of two stuffed toys, either Bunny or Kitty-Cat. We packed them all in a blue nylon Enfamil bag and took it wherever we went.

Packing that bag seems simple, but it wasn't. Since they slept with their comfort items, we couldn't pack them until right before we left. If I set the bag down, the kids would find their comfort item, take it out, and I wouldn't notice until it was too late.

As Jon put the kids in the car, I counted the comfort items one last time to make sure they were all there. I wasn't going to let anything ruin this trip.

Heading down the highway, I could see it was still overcast. "You're sure it's not supposed to rain?" I asked Jon again.

"Nope, they said it was not going to rain."

I wanted to believe him, but forty miles into the drive, the sky darkened ominously.

"Tell me it is not going to rain."

"Kate, it is not going to rain. They said it wasn't going to rain."

Two hours into the drive, the unthinkable happened. It started to rain.

"Jon, it's raining! Now what do we do?"

"What do you want to do?"

I hoped and prayed it wasn't raining at the zoo. We had spent so long researching this trip, packing the van, and getting the kids' hopes up; I couldn't see turning around when maybe it would all blow over.

"Let's keep going."

An hour later, we pulled into the parking lot of the National Zoo, and it was still raining.

"Now what?" Jon asked.

It was pouring at this point. "Let's just make the best of it. If we see three animals and then leave, at least we saw three animals."

We parked and unloaded that huge stroller, which of course meant standing in the rain while we attached the front wheel. When we unloaded the kids, I tried not to make a big deal out of the rain because I didn't want them to get upset. After all, it is just water.

Jon raced to the entrance with the stroller, avoiding the deepest puddles. I ran behind, trying not to get hit with the spray. No question about it—we were going to get wet. "Jon, when we get inside let's see if we can buy some of those rain ponchos." I was determined to help the kids have the best time possible. We took cover in the first shop we saw. "Do you sell rain ponchos?" I asked the girl behind the counter.

"I'm sorry, we're all out. We sold the last one about twenty minutes ago."

My kids in trash bags. What a sight, huh?

It was probably a good thing. I was willing to spend the money, but we couldn't have afforded ten anyway. Then I had an idea. In front of us was a food vendor huddling under his hut to keep dry.

"Excuse me, do you have a roll of trash bags?"

"Uh, yeah. Why?"

"Could you give me ten of them? I'll pay you."

"No, lady, you can just take them," he said as he tore off ten plastic bags.

Growing up, my grandma had taught me a trick; if you poke head and armholes into the trash bag, it's almost like having a rain poncho. One by one, Jon and I dressed each of the kids into a clear trash bag and tucked it around them. Then Jon and I put ours on. It wasn't a perfect solution, but it helped. All morning we had walked around in trash bags and hid under trees and shelters. We spent a long time watching the elephants because they were indoors. We knew we looked ridiculous, but we didn't care. We wanted our kids to experience the zoo like kids in normal-sized families did.

But I had forgotten again that we weren't a normal family. Our first shows had aired and people were starting to recognize us from TV. With the size of our group and our trash-bag ponchos we weren't exactly inconspicuous. Jon noticed people were staring. As word traveled around the zoo, we began to see people taking pictures — not of the animals — but of us. By the time we got to the panda exhibit (a rare display; most zoos in America don't have pandas) we found more people staring and taking pictures of our family than of the pandas! It's actually quite uncomfortable to be in a zoo and find people treating you like the exhibit. I imagined the conversations around us: "Mom, after we see the pandas, can we go see that TV family in the trash bags?" I started to sympathize with the animals.

By lunchtime, we'd had enough and we headed to the parking lot. Back in the van, we stripped wet clothes off the kids and put on dry outfits from the stash in the van. Jon took his wet shirt off and thought he had an extra clean one. But when he pulled it out of his backpack, he discovered something had spilled on it. We distributed the lunches and took off for the long drive home—with Jon driving shirtless.

Just outside of Washington, I yelled at Jon to stop. "Look! There's an organic grocery store." I was always searching for organic foods and there weren't organic stores near us. The kids were dry and happy and Jon was fine with stopping. I think the fact that there was a Starbucks across the street didn't hurt either.

"Go in and see what you can find," he said. "When you get back, I'll throw my jacket on and run across the street and get us each a coffee." The rain had subsided a bit, but I was still wet and the coffee sounded good (but when doesn't it sound good to me?).

"I'll be right back!" I was only in the store ten minutes, but as I came out the door I could see it was raining harder. On my way to the van, I noticed something disturbing; no one was in the driver's seat! My first thought was that Jon was in the back with the kids, but as I rounded the corner I saw Jon standing in the parking lot, drenched! He had a horrified expression on his face.

"What's wrong?"

"Look!" he said and opened the van door.

The smell hit before I saw it. Vomit. Vomit on Alexis who was in her seat and crying hysterically. Vomit on her car seat. Chunks dripping onto the floor mats.

The smell was overpowering. So was the sound. All of the kids were wailing because it smelled so bad.

"I … I don't know what to say," said Jon.

More important, he didn't know what to do. He was paralyzed.

I grabbed Alexis and handed her to Jon. "Use the rain to wash her off." He started stripping off her clothes. I reached under the seat for the lemon-scented wipes and tried to clean up her car seat. I wanted to take it apart but couldn't because we were hours from home and she still had to ride in it.

Vomit was in every crack and crevice. The kids screamed and gagged. The heat and humidity combined with the putrid smell made me nauseous. We couldn't open the windows because of the rain. I was worried more kids would start throwing up, so I handed them the only thing I had. "Hold the wipe up to your nose and breathe through it." I hoped the lemon scent would somehow mask the smell, but if it didn't, at least it would give them something to do.

As Jon stood in the rain, Alexis wearing only a diaper, sniffled in his arms. We were out of outfits, so we wrapped her in a blanket before putting her in her seat. Dripping wet once again, Jon and I got back into the van and looked at each other helplessly.

The kids fell asleep on the way home. I don't know who was more ecstatic to pull into the driveway, Jon or I. Despite all our planning and preparation, we couldn't have predicted the things that went wrong that day.

Had we known before we started, we never would have continued with the trip. But looking back, I am glad we had that experience. In some warped way, that horrendous day at the zoo gave us the confidence to attempt more outings. Though it was one of our worst trips ever, Jon and I agreed that if we could handle that we could handle anything.

By the time July rolled around, we were getting more adventurous. Grandmom turned sixty and we took Cara, Mady, Leah, and Joel to her surprise party. After that we had promised the kids another outing, but it was too hot to take the bus very far. We needed a backup plan or Mady and Cara would be the ones melting down. We needed to go somewhere that didn't cost a lot of money and that we could handle logistically. That place was Chocolate World.

Chocolate World is Hershey's visitor center, and only a fifteen-minute drive from our house. They had shops and a factory tour—the perfect place to take the kids. Jon and I began thinking logistics.

We wouldn't be able to take strollers because of the stairs. The babies could walk, but they had a tendency to roam, especially Alexis and Joel. We needed to find another adult to go with us. A phone call later, our friends Karl and Kristen agreed to come along. We made plans to leave our house at 6:00 p.m.

At 5:15, the skies darkened and it looked like rain. We loaded the kids into the bus early, which turned out to be a wise decision. While we waited for Karl and Kristen, it started storming wildly, complete with hail. Jon and the kids looked out the van windows as I prayed we would be safe. From the car, we watched as the lights in the neighborhood flashed and then went out. Without electricity, we couldn't do anything at home, so when Karl and Kristen arrived we proceeded as planned.

I'm so glad we did! The kids had a great time. They were yelling with glee at the talking cows. And because they walked, we didn't draw too much attention (though Jon says he saw people counting). It felt so "normal" to ride the rides together as a family.

After Chocolate World, we went to an ice cream shop the kids call the Purple Place. This was a big step for an all-natural organic momma whose idea of a sugary treat was an animal cracker! We fed the kids vanilla soft serve. It was so cute to see the little kids saying "bite-bite" when they wanted more.

By the time we got home three and a half hours later, the power was still out. Jon grabbed a flashlight and together we gave the kids sponge baths on the dining room table. I washed and passed them to Jon who dried and dressed them. The kids were sugared up, so they just chased each other in the dark.

Surprisingly, I was the one who was calm throughout the ordeal and Jon was the one who was grouchy. For me, it felt like a small victory; I was learning to roll with the situation even when I didn't have control. Fortunately, the power came on before we put the kids to bed. I fell asleep that night appreciating how we were learning to make it work — even when it didn't always work the way we wanted it to. It felt like another baby step into the normal world. The kids weren't the only ones growing; I was growing too.

At the parade on our favorite summer holiday.

Two days later was our favorite summer holiday: the Fourth of July. Jon and I always loved the parade in Wyomissing, and we planned to take the kids. We had them up by 7:00 and eating breakfast by 7:30. By 8:38, we were in the bus and on the road. It felt like quite an accomplishment for two tired parents.

Once there, we met some friends, found a place along the route, and parked the stroller so the little kids would have a good view of the parade. I passed out balloons and flags and was getting ready to sit down when I realized we had a total of six adults.

"Jon, what if we let the kids out of their stroller? We could put one adult in charge of each kid."

"I don't know. It's easier if we just leave them in the stroller."

"Yes, it's easier," I agreed. "But when do we ever do what's easy?"

Jon agreed. I passed a kid to each set of adult arms. Once the parade started, the little kids quickly learned from Mady and Cara that when candy is thrown your way, you run to pick it up. It made me so happy to see that my babies could experience the parade like normal two-year-olds! I think it also relieved some of my guilt about the sacrifices they had to make because of the size and makeup of our family.

After the parade, we made our way to the picnic area where I spread a blanket and fed them lunch. The kids had peanut butter crackers, cantaloupe, and cheese. They were so sweet as they sat and ate, and I was proud of their behavior. It reassured me to know we could take them out in public without an incident.

That night, we had a picnic dinner at home in our backyard. I put the babies in swimmies and we set up the sprinkler balls. The girls donned their swimsuits and off they went. I must have been tired, because I let the babies get filthy dirty and I never do that. But they loved it! When we were ready to come in, two of them had poopy swimmies, which complicated things a bit, but I washed them all down with utility towels and then sent them upstairs to Daddy for a much-needed bath. Together we got the kids bathed, lotioned, and dressed, and they went to bed with no complaints. We were quite a team!

It was such a fun day. And at the end of it, I felt like we'd accomplished something important. I had been able to have a good time, and I know the kids had a great time too. My organization once again saved us! It got me thinking: I might be up for the organizational challenge of Disney next summer. Nanny Joan and Terry had offered to meet us at Disney to help, and for the first time I thought it might be a good idea.

Obviously, I was growing in confidence. We were also growing as a family, taking steps outside of the house, and exploring new things.

❋ ❋ ❋

Before we could attempt a trip to Disney, we needed a few more experiences under our belt. We went to the "Purple Place" a few more
times and learned that pulling directly up to the deck meant we
could unload the kids without needing another adult. Cara and Mady
helped Jon with the little kids while I placed the orders.

Aaden taking his sisters for a ride at Cocoa Castle.

In mid-July, we attempted the Cocoa Castle, a playground near the recreation center in Hershey. Built over fifteen years ago, the wooden play structure had stairs, slides, bridges, and other games. Using the lesson from the Purple Place, Jon pulled the bus as close to the entrance as possible to drop them off. I was nervous about watching eight kids by myself so I offered to park the car while Jon went in with the kids.

For the most part the kids stayed in a pack, and I snapped pictures as they ran through the playground. Unfortunately, we couldn't let them play long, maybe twenty minutes, because Jon noticed dark clouds looming. When I tried to herd them into the bus, Collin threw himself on the ground and absolutely refused to go. Oh, it was lovely! But even with the tantrum Jon and I were glad we had taken them, and proud to learn that we could do it on our own.

A few weeks later, we decided to take the family to Friendly's restaurant in Hershey. By this time our show had been on TV for a while and we were beginning to be recognized more frequently. I learned that if I called ahead, they could put us to one side where we'd cause less attention.

Before we left, Cara packed the comfort bag all by herself and very willingly. She did a great job and it was nice to have an extra set of hands getting things ready.

At the restaurant, we had a little trouble getting the kids out of the bus. Remember the dog licking my ankles and the rude lady? This was the trip. Once inside, I ordered food immediately because I wasn't sure how the kids would do with the wait. Cara got a hot dog and fries. I ordered three chicken fingers kids' meals—some with fries and some with broccoli. When the plates arrived I divided it all up and gave the other seven some of everything.

The kids did awesome. Jon sat next to Alexis, with Mady and Aaden across from him. Joel was on the end of the table. I sat with Hannah next to me. Leah was on the other end of the table, and Cara and Collin were across from me. I showed Hannah how to get

Enjoying a family meal at a restaurant in Georgia on our way to Florida.

napkins and she was able to get them for all the kids. Both Hannah and Leah were able to handle ketchup with their fries.

After dinner, we went back to our favorite playground—Cocoa Castle—and this time we were able to stay longer. They played until it was time to leave and everyone went willingly. I was so proud of them. "Good job, guys!" I said.

"Good job, Mommy!" said Hannah.

That was so sweet to hear. Especially because I felt like I had done a good job. I had spent the day cleaning and then I had the rare privilege of not having to make dinner and clean up the mess. When we got home, all we had to do was give the kids a bath and put them to bed. Oh, how marvelous!

Going anywhere outside of the house was a treat for the kids. I remember a trip to Target right around that time. Jon and I each put four kids in a cart. We got the usual stares and conversations, but the kids didn't notice. They were all looking up at the shelves lined with colors and shapes. It just wasn't normal for them to go to a store like that, in fact, for some of them, it may have been their first visit. Our kids were always so good in public because they didn't get to go out very often. They were too amazed at everything they saw to act up. As we loaded the kids in the car, Leah started fussing and tried to tell me something. "No home, Mommy. No home, Mommy!"

She didn't want to leave!

"Are you having fun, Leah?" I asked.

She nodded her head.

"Okay, how about we drive around and you can look out the window?"

She seemed happy with that idea. She is really easy, let me tell you.

By September 2006, we had the basics down. We could do family outings without too much trouble. One Sunday we took the kids to Applebee's, calling ahead to arrange seating.

When we arrived, we used our newest (and easiest!) way of moving: we walked in holding hands. People were awed — actually staring with open mouths — as we walked to our table. One lady and her husband at the bar both seemed fascinated with us; they had a curious expression as they watched our every move. They also had a baby with them. I couldn't help but wonder what they were thinking as they watched our little parade.

We got everyone seated rather quickly and in a relatively organized fashion. The waitress said we could have two free kids' meals with their kids' club and she gave me a card for each child for a free meal on their birthday. The staff went out of their way to be kind and we so appreciated their generosity and help.

At some point, a new waitress came over to our table. "Here, this is for you," she said, handing Jon a five-dollar bill.

"What's this for?" he asked.

"I was working the take-out section and a woman picking up her food saw your van. She asked me if a couple with twins and sextuplets was inside. I told her yes. Then she gave me the money and asked me to give it to you."

Jon and I were surprised and touched by her kindness.

The kids ate well and were very well behaved. I think we impressed the people around us. I don't want to brag, but I was impressed myself. The Applebee's employees all stood and waved as we left. The kids said "bye-bye." It was too cute!

When we got into the van, Jon put his hand out and we slapped a high-five.

"That was cake!" he said.

I thought so too. When we first started going out with the kids I never imagined a day we'd think it was easy.

I think we appreciated those experiences more than "normal" families because we had to work so much harder to make them happen. Sometimes people would say, "Oh, my gosh, I can't believe you took all the kids and did that." And I understood. Pure exhaustion followed every excursion. Not only because of the planning and execution, but also because of the emotional energy of constantly being on high alert. It would have been much easier to stay home, but we wanted our kids to have opportunities to experience the world outside our home.

I grew up in a house with four siblings, and I don't ever remember being in a restaurant with my family. Until I was an adult, I didn't even know how to order off of a menu! I didn't want that for my kids. We couldn't afford to eat out often, but we did it as often as we could.

After the dinner at Applebee's, we went to the Cocoa Castle. As we pulled in, Hannah yelled, "Castle! Hi Castle!" Somehow, that made all our effort worth it. My kids were braver than they were at the beginning of the summer. They were eagerly embracing and engaging the world around them. Though it was exhausting for Jon and me, that's why we did it.

When your kids can get through a meal in a restaurant and the waitress compliments their behavior, you know you've done something right. Yes, we've had those meals where Mady (or any of the kids for that matter) melted down and Jon took them to the car to deal with it, but that's part of growing too.

We pushed through. We started with church and took on more challenges over time. Each trip taught us something that we applied to the planning and logistics of the next one. Looking back, I can see that it would have been easy to allow our fears to keep us inside our house, but by tackling that fear head on, we were able to expand our comfort zone. That first trip to the zoo wasn't a treat, but it was a confidence builder and formed the foundation for the trips we took later and enjoyed. We didn't let the bad times stop us from trying again. We learned that anything was possible, not because of the right preparation, but because of the right attitude. That's the bottom line. It takes a lot of energy, but if you want something enough, it can be done.

4

DEAR JESUS

Starting from the time the little kids turned two, my faith started to grow and became personal to me, and I began writing prayers—in essence, my own letters to God—in my journal as an expression of faith.

When the little kids were born, we just needed God to show up and provide for us. It wasn't until two years later that I realized and understood that he wanted a unique and personal relationship with each of us. He created each of us uniquely and we all matter to him— our needs, wants, and desires are all important to God. I could have done fertility treatments for years, and if it wasn't his plan for us to have twins and sextuplets, we wouldn't have had them—or any kids for that matter. This was God's perfect plan for us, and I was awed by the realization that he had a plan for my life and for my family. He uniquely picked me to be the mother of these exact kids, and I needed to trust that his plan was the best plan for me. Accordingly,

I needed to adjust "my plan" with his perfect plan — even when it felt exhausting (which was pretty much all the time).

My faith was always important to me but it was never more important than when I had to depend on God to provide for my family. I prayed for little things and big things; praying made it possible for me not to worry anymore. I asked him to lead my prayers because I truly didn't want anything that God didn't want for me. He never failed us. His provision was so clear, we could not deny it. Every single day we saw a miracle.

One of my very favorite stories — and one that I mention frequently — began on Christmas Eve in 2006 when my brother and sisters and their families came over to celebrate the holiday with us. After dinner, as we were doing dishes, my sister Kendra was talking about a family at her church with four kids, whose Christmas was going to be difficult for them because the dad had been unemployed for over a year.

As I handed her a dish to dry, I got a sick feeling in my stomach and thought, "Been there, done that. I do not ever want to go back to that time in our lives."

After they left, I could not stop thinking about that family. I knew God was saying I needed to write them a check. I remember arguing with him for a few days, but he wouldn't let up and even put a number in my head. Finally, out of exasperation, I called my sister to get the family's name and address. I wrote out the check right then and there and ran to the mailbox. (You would run too if you had six two-year-olds ready to disassemble your house on a moment's notice.) When I opened up the mailbox, I saw another envelope inside with a bow on it. It hadn't come through the mail system. In my best time-saving skills, I ripped open the envelope as I was running back to the house. I literally almost fell over when I saw what was inside: A gift card for Sam's Club in the exact amount I had just written the check for.

This is only one example of the many times God has provided

perfectly. We could not deny his work in our house. Chance could not have put that envelope in our mailbox with the gift card. In the exact amount. On that exact day. This still amazes me.

❊ ❊ ❊

One day when Mady was five, she was playing in the basement. She's naturally inquisitive, so she's always asking me questions. After a few questions about Jesus, she said matter-of-factly: "So Mommy, tell me how I can go to heaven."

I was a little taken aback since she was only five, and I have never pressured any of my kids into this decision. But she seemed to understand what she was asking, so I explained that she had to ask Jesus into her heart.

Mady answered, "Oh, I'd like to do that."

Right there in the middle of our toy explosion, she accepted Jesus into her heart. Cara sat back and watched, but her turn didn't come until a year later.

One stormy summer night, we were sitting down to have dinner and Hannah was singing, "B-I-B-I-B."

I didn't have the heart to tell her it was B-I-B-L-E. "Who's going to say thank you to Jesus?" I asked.

"I will!" Mady said.

Cara said, "We should pray for Daddy that he is safe. It looks scary outside." Jon hadn't come home from work yet and the storm looked like it was getting worse. And then she added softly, "Mommy. I want to ask Jesus into my heart after dinner."

"Oh, Cara, of course!" I said through tears as I bent down to give her a hug.

After dinner, the girls took the little kids downstairs to play while I cleaned up. Cara came back up after a few minutes and said, "Remember, I want to ask Jesus into my heart." I put down the cups I was clearing and took her into our bedroom and led her in the salvation prayer.

"Dear Jesus, I know I'm a sinner. Please forgive me. Please come into my heart. Thank you for dying on the cross for my sins so I can live forever with you as you promised. In Jesus' name, amen."

Apart from seeing your kids born healthy, there is nothing sweeter than seeing them accept Jesus into their heart.

❀ ❀ ❀

One of the biggest ways I put my faith to the test during this time was the decision to quit my job. In April of 2005 I had started working again—one day a week as a nurse at an outpatient dialysis clinic. Every Saturday I worked a double shift (sixteen hours). At our old house, work was only five minutes away, but it was an hour away from Elizabethtown. I left at five a.m., started work at six a.m., and worked until ten p.m., so I didn't get home until eleven at night. I frequently asked Jon to pray for my drive home as I was exhausted after that long day and often dozed off on the road. It was scary!

As brutal as such a long workday was, it really was a great setup for us. I was grateful for the opportunity, as such flexibility in a job is hard to come by.

Every Friday I prepped all day for Saturday. I left notes, schedules, and meals, and Jon was home with the kids all day on Saturday. I used to say, "In our house, mom or dad, it doesn't make a difference." Jon was a very hands-on dad, and our kids didn't prefer a parent—one was as good as the other.

By mid–2006 I started to feel that I needed to quit my job to be home more. We were trying to fit in filming time, and I didn't want to miss every Saturday. The guilt of not being with my family on the weekends weighed heavily on me.

I prayed constantly for my girls, who were in first grade. I asked God to protect them and to bring them home safely every day. I prayed that God would keep them innocent from all evil at school and to feel his love around them. I wanted them to shine for him!

But even with all my prayers, I still missed my big girls. They were gone to school during the week, and I was working on the weekends. I prayed that God would make a way for me to be home at least until the six were in school full time. Besides, Jon and I needed to have some lazy Saturdays as a family to let a little steam out of the pressure cooker of life. "Please, Lord," I said, "please! I want to be here!"

Soon I felt like God was saying, "Okay. Quit. Trust me on this."

As much as I wanted to do what he asked, I ignored him. We really needed my paycheck, and I couldn't see how we could make it work without that income. I continued to wrestle with this issue. I really wanted to be a stay-at-home mom, but the financial part didn't seem to line up with my desire. I knew God was urging me to quit and trust in him—and I wanted to listen—but I wasn't quite ready to let go and let him handle our finances.

Things came to a head when my new boss wanted me to work double shifts December 23 and 24. Not only did he want me to work on Christmas Eve, it was also a Saturday and Sunday—and I was hired only to work Saturdays. When I told him I couldn't, he didn't agree. After all, he wasn't the one who hired me, and he needed to do his job by scheduling enough staff. But for me, as I already had been wrestling with the idea of quitting, I knew this was God's way of telling me the time had come. I could trust him. He had always met our needs. Everything had always been taken care of.

I spent time praying, journaling, and reading my devotions as I thought about my options. God was urging me to quit. Jon really wanted me to quit too, which was amazing. And now my boss was making it almost impossible for me not to quit. All this time I had asked God to make it very clear to me what to do, and now he had. I thought about the Israelites entering the Promised Land, and reminded myself that not trusting in God always prevents us from receiving his best.

Sometimes I need answers to be written in the sky in order for me to obey and trust God; but he seems to meet me where I am in my trust in him — or lack thereof. I was still scared to give up my income, but had finally decided do so, since God made it very obvious I needed to.

So finally I heard the words, "I quit," come out of my mouth. The next time I talked to my boss, I told him my last day would be December 9.

"Okay, I have you down for December 9 and 23," he said, "and then I'll take you off the schedule."

"No," I said, staying firm. "December 9 is my very last day."

While I was worried and scared to be out of work, I knew God would always provide. I also felt thrilled to be doing what God wanted me to do. When I told Cara and Mady I wouldn't be working anymore, Cara lunged toward me and held on for a while, hugging me very tightly as though I had just given her a toy she had been begging for. She confirmed it: I had definitely made the right decision.

Still, while paying bills later that week, I got nervous again, worried that maybe I didn't do the right thing. But in my devotions that night, I read this: "To claim that prayer will always be answered in the very way and for the particular thing that we desire, is presumption. God is too wise to err, and too good to withhold any good thing from them that walk uprightly."

With that in mind, I put my fears aside and decided firmly to continue to rely on the Lord for our needs. He would pull us through, I knew, because I was obeying him by staying home with my family. And I was thankful for the opportunity he had given me.

About a year later, Jon and I were invited to speak at a church in Mississippi. I worked closely Vanessa who had arranged the trip, and while I was there, she was sharing with me that she was pregnant with her third child and wanted to stay at home with her kids. I told her my story about how I struggled with the same dilemma.

Three months later it was so rewarding to receive this email from her:

Kate,

  Thank you so much for sharing your story with me. I quit my job and am now a stay-at-home mom, and I couldn't be happier. God has provided for all of our needs just like you said he would. Thanks again for encouraging me.

Vanessa

❈ ❈ ❈

My kids are constantly teaching me about faith through their own wonder and amazement and acceptance. One night at the dinner table, Mady prayed for our meal: "Thank you, Jesus, for putting this food in our cabinets so Mommy could make us dinner."

I was blown away at her choice of words and understanding, so I asked her where she came up with that prayer.

In an almost condescending tone, she said, "Well, Jesus *did* put it there!"

Of course. Silly me.

Another evening as I was preparing dinner in the kitchen, Joel walked in and announced, "Oh, Mommy! Look at the sky! How did it get like that?"

Looking at the sunset with its full display of oranges, blues, pinks, and purples, I responded, "Jesus painted it."

"How?"

"Not with a paintbrush, but he made the sky and decorated it."

"Oh!"

The next night brought another gorgeous sunset, and Joel once again walked in and looked out the window. "Look, Mommy. Jesus painted the sky again!"

In our busy stressful lives, we often don't remember to look at sunsets. Our kids often have to point out the simple wonders of living. Since then, whenever I see a sunset like that, no matter where I'm at or who I'm with, I have to say out loud, "Oh look, Jesus painted the sky again."

❄ ❄ ❄

Jon and I had planned a trip to California for our first church speaking event in November, and as the date approached I began to feel nervous. Flying is not exactly my favorite thing to do. What if we crashed? I couldn't bear the idea of not being around for the kids and not seeing them grow up. I spent some time praying that God would protect us the entire trip and reunite our family on Monday when we returned. Just saying things like, "I know you love us, Lord, and I know you are in control. I will trust you!" calmed my heart. Putting myself in God's hands was the safest thing I could do.

It's probably a good thing I learned to pray like this, because traveling unbeknownst to me at the time was going to become a big part of my life. Jon and I had two more speaking trips coming up in the beginning of 2007, and I kept on praying for our safety, and more. These were important trips, and I was thankful for the opportunity to show God's love to the world. I prayed that we would glorify God in all that we said and did. I prayed for our children's safety, and for them to be happy and feel safe and loved while we were away. I prayed that Jon and I would be able to relax and enjoy our trips so that when we returned we would be more loving and patient parents. I also prayed that Jon and I would reconnect and remember how much we love each other. "Thank you for this never-boring journey you have chosen to send us on," I prayed. I still thank God for that.

My travels continued, and my prayers did too. I was learning to pray for so much more than myself. I asked God to let his love shine through me as I spoke at different events and venues, and to let me be an example of his love to all who met me.

❄ ❄ ❄

Prayer and parenting seem to go hand in hand. God knows — and I tell him constantly — that I have always wanted us to be parents who serve him and who teach our children how to love him and each other. I could not do that without prayer. "Lord, make me kind and loving and patient and caring," I wrote in my journal. "Help my children to know that I love them and that everything I do is for them!"

Marriage is the same way: we can't do it without prayer. Some days marriage was easy, but when life got stressful and the weight of the world seemed to fall on me, it was all I could do to cry out, "Lord, deliver me from myself and Jon from himself! Please help us to love each other and help me to keep my mouth shut, especially when I am tired and irritable!" I think I know now just how important those types of prayers were—and are, for every marriage.

Overall, some of my favorite prayers were the ones I took straight from Scripture or from meaningful songs and hymns, like, "Strength for today and bright hope for tomorrow. Great is thy faithfulness, Lord unto me." These prayers seemed to speak for me when I couldn't come up with the words to say myself. I love that there are different ways to communicate with Jesus. My biggest prayer will continue to be that my children have a strong relationship with God and learn to rely on him in every situation.

Letter to Alexis

Dear Alexis,

My "Precious Moments" girl, you were named before you existed! After Cara and Mady were born, Daddy and I agreed our next girl (if we had one!) would be named Alexis. In addition, I always knew that Faith would be your middle name because I had faith that even with our fertility issues, we would be able to have another baby. I've always loved how perfect Alexis Faith is together!

While I desired to have a third baby, it was a complete shock to learn that I was going to have seven more babies at once! As you know, our seventh baby now lives in heaven with Jesus and went there when she was very tiny. You especially talk about "our other baby" often. We imagine what her name would have been. Emma Rose? Or Ella Rose? (We have agreed it was a girl).

To be honest, it took Mommy quite awhile to accept the idea of so many babies at once; but over time, I was able to embrace my destiny and put my best mommy efforts to the task of keeping you growing and healthy until you were big enough to be born safely. After you were born, the task was strangely similar. You, Hannah, Aaden, Collin, Leah, and Joel were born prematurely, as predicted, at 29 weeks and 5 days. A normal pregnancy lasts about 40 weeks, so your early birth meant you came about 10 weeks too soon.

I'll never forget the first time I saw your precious teeny

face! I managed to visit you in the neonatal unit eight hours after your birth. You were in the incubator closest to the door. I lifted the cover and saw your golden blonde hair and your closed Asian eyes. I smiled because you were the first of my children that even hinted at a resemblance of me. I also had blonde hair as a little girl!

Your tiny pink cheeks and lips made me cry. You were perfect in every way—just small. Two pounds eleven point five ounces to be exact. I was instantly overcome with love for you. Your brothers and sisters were spread throughout the NICU and it made me feel sad that you were, for the first time ever, separated from your womb mates. I whispered to you, "Hi Alexis, it's Mommy. I love you! I'm sorry you have to be here. I did my best to keep you safe as long as I could. Rest baby. Grow strong so I can take you home soon!"

The next year was filled with many bottles and diaper changes. But it was mostly a year filled with people helping and inundating our tiny house at each feeding time. I know you remember who fed you most, Alexis: Your Nana Janet, who was the comedic relief during most eight p.m. feedings. She would tell funny stories to the point where we were all laughing so hard that Janet got worried we were shaking the babies too much. "Oh, these poor babies," she'd say. And of course, that would just make us laugh harder. I credit those bedtime feedings as not only good comedy but also good stress relief.

I often told Janet that I blamed her for making you so goofy and silly, and she readily accepted the "blame"—and loved you so much. She was an ever-present constant in your and your brothers and sisters' lives. You had many chats with Nana over the next few years as she ironed, played or read books with you.

I've watched you grow into a kind and caring little girl. I

have enjoyed the humor you have brought to our family. You have a way of knowing when I need a silly Alexis face to brighten my day. Or even a silly Alexis comment that only you can come up with! Ironically, you earned the nickname "Sassy" from your brothers and sisters. They couldn't say Alexis, so Sassy stuck— mostly, I think, because you just plain were!

When I look at you, I see complete beauty. You have "the face of an angel" as Grandmom used to say. It's a good cover for that naughty side that lurks behind the mischievous twinkle in your eye! I look forward to watching that face—and the rest of you—grow. You have a kindness and empathy for others (and animals!) that I hope you always continue. Remembering that God created every person, no matter their appearance, occupation, abilities, or inabilities, and developing the desire to see others the way God sees them will help you to navigate life successfully. I have not always possessed the skills to see others this way. In recent years, as life has exposed our family to so many people, places, and experiences, I have been more able to love and befriend others more readily, but it took me awhile. I admire your warmth and acceptance of anyone who walks into your life. Never lose sight of this gift that seems to come more naturally to you.

Over the last few years, our family life has changed a lot. I want you to know that one thing that will never change is my love for you. Although these changes are confusing and quite upsetting to you now, I'll willingly help you understand why someday. Always know that above all else your needs and the needs of your brothers and sisters are my first priority.

Work hard, Alexis. Take the hard road and finish whatever you start! You will develop a deep confidence in yourself if you always do your best—even if it's difficult.

I love it that you want to "get a baby," as you constantly say; but be sure you first graduate from college and get married ("get a husband," as you say). These have been my continual instructions to you and your sisters.

Whatever you choose to do in life, I will support you. I am your biggest cheerleader and will be by your side always helping you. I wish for you a happy life—one that brings you a satisfying education, career, and family. Come to me when you need advice, help, instructions, or just a good listener. I'm here for you—today and all of your tomorrows.

Love forever and always, no matter what,

Mommy

5

BEHIND THE SCENES

Long before anyone had heard of us, Jon put together our family website, which he worked on in the evenings in the closet where his computer was. We were proud of our family and were happy to provide progress reports in response to the many inquiries from the interested and supportive public.

We had been doing local news reports because we felt we owed the community an update. I could picture the little old ladies my grandma's age saying, "I wonder what happened to those babies." However, the reporters always tied cute little bows on the story — this cute little couple, with cute little twins, had six cute little babies — without talking about the struggles. Jon was unemployed for a year, we were struggling to make ends meet, and everyday life was isolating and difficult with eight kids under the age of six. We weren't complaining; we just felt misrepresented. Jon and I didn't feel like that "cute little couple."

One day we received an email through our family website from a production company. I called them to find out what they were about. The production company owner's motto was that he made real TV for people to understand people better. That was all I needed to hear. We felt like we were misunderstood at this time—we were just parents with fertility issues who got more than we bargained for, but we were determined to make the best of it.

The production company wanted to make a one-hour documentary with the Discovery Health Channel. I personally remembered watching documentaries about multiples and found them fascinating, so I thought others might be interested in our story. Our main benefit was that six to nine months of our lives would be on a DVD for us to show our kids someday. The idea of capturing our lives on film at this time was very enticing since we were too busy to do it ourselves. Sign us up!

Cara, Mady, Hannah, and Leah playing in the snow.

It turned out that there were additional benefits besides the family footage. In addition to covering a dinner out, the production company offered to cover our bill when we filmed at Sam's Club, and they purchased snow boots for the children when we picked out a Christmas tree. This helped us immensely.

During our first hour special on the Discovery Health Channel, I had shown my ugly "jowls of a dog" belly because I knew, had I been on the other side, I would have been interested in what a belly looked like after having sextuplets. A plastic surgeon and his wife saw the episode and contacted the network to offer me a free tummy tuck. I was standing in my bedroom when I heard the news, and I screamed at the top of my lungs. When I finished screaming, I could not remember the phone number of any of my friends or family — or Jon! — to share the news. I was speechless (which doesn't happen often).

What an opportunity! I would say a dream come true, but I hadn't even dared to have that dream. Lots of logistics and expenses had to be figured out before this was a sure thing — like who was going to help take care of the kids, how I was going to be able to miss work, how I could recover after major surgery with eight small children. An amazing opportunity for sure, but would it become a reality?

Then the production company stepped in to say that they were interested in making another hour special and would like to film this as part of the show. They offered to assist in the additional logistical and financial concerns. This dream was becoming a reality.

Just prepping for being away during the surgery was a feat in itself. At the time, I could barely leave the house for work for sixteen hours without major planning. I cooked for two days straight in order to have two weeks of meals during the recovery process after the surgery. Even the decision of who took which kids, which kids got along best together took careful planning. We ended up splitting our kids up between five different homes of friends and family, whom we were so grateful for. But that meant I needed to pack five different suitcases, write fives sets of detailed instructions, and spend a day and a half dropping everyone off. Two days before we left, Jon drove four hours each way to meet my friend Jamie who was taking Cara and Mady. The day before we left, we spent the entire day playing school bus as we dropped off the little kids at four different homes.

It felt very odd, as we headed to New York for the surgery without any kids. This was the first time Jon and I had traveled anywhere alone without any kids since I was pregnant with Cara and Mady, and we were strangely looking forward to it. On the night before surgery as we were settling into the hotel, it finally occurred to me that I was going to have a major procedure and for the first time I started to get nervous. I had been so busy planning for it that I hadn't had time to really think about having surgery until that point.

The surgery itself went well, though there was more repair work done than originally anticipated. The muscles were so stretched apart, my abs were ripped down the middle, and there was a four inch gap. The surgeon sewed the muscles back together, removed $1-1/2$ pounds of skin, and repaired two hernias.

Because of all the work that was done, the pain afterward made my C-section pain pale in comparison. My muscles spasmed for a full week.

A week later, when I finally arrived home from my surgery, I walked into the little kids' room to find them in their cribs. Alexis didn't quite recognize me because while away I had also changed the color of my hair. She kept saying, "Hi Mommy. Hi Mommy. Hi Mommy." She was oh so adorable.

I had missed them so much! And to say that was an understatement since I had never been away from them that long before.

Taking so much time to recover from the surgery was tough and took quite a bit of creativity. I wasn't allowed to lift the kids for two weeks but still had to take care of them. I had put the sides of their cribs down and taught them how to climb out onto a stool, changed them on the floor, and had them climb into their high chairs.

Two weeks after the surgery I slowly started to get back into a regular routine. I still couldn't believe my belly was on its way to looking normal again.

As you can see, the fringe benefits affiliated with making the second hour special helped us out immensely, and in this case, made it possible for a dream to come true. An additional bonus was that we had yet a second hour of memories captured on DVD.

By the time we signed up to do the television series, we had been filming for a year already. We liked the routine, our kids loved the crew members, and we loved being able to work at home and travel as a family—a win-win all around. Jon and I were in agreement that this was a great opportunity for all of us.

It wasn't until much later that the price to pay for giving up our privacy became evident—as no one could have predicted how well our show would do.

Everybody talks about saving for college for their kids, but it was almost laughable to us with eight children, who would all be attending at the same time. It's definitely a daunting dream to send them all to college, but every time we could, we put a little away. Even though we didn't have a lot of money, we were not in debt. So when we signed on to do the series (one season at that time), our primary goal was to put the money toward providing for the future of our children, even though we knew that the amount wouldn't make a dent in eight college funds. I know there's nothing wrong with working your way through college—that's what I did even though I still needed financial assistance from my grandparents. But we wanted to be sure they had the opportunity to go to college, and we didn't want money to be what kept them from going. If we had an only child, we'd pay for her college, so why couldn't we do it for eight?

❈ ❈ ❈

There was more to filming than viewers got to see. Filming was flexible and the crew worked around our family schedule. We filmed anywhere from two hours to six hours a day, and from one to three days a week. The majority of the interviews at the end of the episodes were taped at night after the kids were in bed, since that was the only time the house was quiet. Those interviews were fun times where Jon and I would laugh and hang out with the crew. We drank coffee and ate jelly beans and often continued hanging out long after our interviews were completed. This was our way of spending time with co-workers, and we enjoyed our working relationship with them.

Leah helps by "clapping" the marker during a television shoot.

We worked hard to keep a steady, familiar crew to create a personal intimate environment. We made it a point to meet and get to know each person before they became a part of our film crew so they weren't bodies behind cameras; they were people with a friendship and familiarity with our family.

When the cameras were off, the crew and the kids played together. They would give piggy back rides, play games, stack blocks, and watch skits Mady and Cara put on for them. The kids even had nicknames for each of them—Stinky, Meatball, Wave, and Jen

Little. When they would arrive for filming, the kids would run and greet them with hugs. Then they would start in on the stories they had saved up to tell crew.

Mike, the sound guy, used his furry boom mic as a toy for them, and Collin once used a long weed as his own boom mic.

In addition our kids had a rare opportunity to be a part of something that provided financial benefits, enjoyable life experiences, and family memories. We were amazed at how well it all worked!

6

A MIRACLE A DAY

Our family experienced firsthand God's provision for us more times than we can count—groceries came exactly when we needed them, we had a "shoe angel" who got us through numerous seasons by providing eight pairs of shoes, we received clothing and even Christmas presents from viewers of our show. Everything was always taken care of.

During our first Christmas on Andrew Avenue, we were getting by but didn't have enough to do anything extra. JoAnn from Georgia sent boxes and boxes of Christmas gifts that she had hand-wrapped for our kids. All I had to do was take them out of the boxes and put them under the tree. JoAnn has sent our kids something each Christmas since—and has since moved on to also helping a quintuplet family. She has never forgotten us and has brought us so much joy as well as relieved so much guilt.

After seeing our first one-hour special, Connie from Ohio emailed me and said she wanted to send our kids each a pair of shoes! She has no idea how much this helped and what her thoughtfulness meant to me. She was our shoe angel. Each season she would email me to find out the kids' shoe sizes. She would then ask me to pick out shoes from online or would copy and paste a few options on email and ask me to pick them. And then she would send us shoes. She even started a shoe club at her church, where a group of women would have coffee and then go pick out shoes for the Gosselin kids. They truly enjoyed shopping for them and my kids were elated to open the packages and see what shoe surprise awaited them.

Lying in front of the freshly decorated Christmas tree.

On the way home from church one Sunday, we had planned to stop by a woman's house. She had seen our hour special on the Discovery Health Channel, contacted me, and asked to meet us; she also said she had a box of things for our family. I checked with Jon and he agreed we should do this. On our way, every single kid fell asleep.

"Kate, are you sure we need to stop by? It's actually peaceful in here for once," Jon said.

"I know, but we told her we would."

"Is it worth going out of our way?"

"It doesn't matter. We need to go since we said we would," I answered.

We pulled up to the house and knocked on the door.

"Thanks so much for stopping by!" the woman said. Her

Opening a gift from a fan!

name was Denise, and she was cheery and kind. She and her husband were our age and had two little girls. "I have a few things for you." She pulled out a box of household supplies and then handed us an

Mady, Hannah, and Cara
with packages.

envelope.

As I looked in, I started to tear up. The envelope was full of gift cards — Target, Walmart, among others — as well as a check. I couldn't believe it. "Thank you so much!" I said to Denise. "You are our miracle today."

Truly at that time, it took a miracle a day.

❋ ❋ ❋

One Sunday night in September 2007, we were eating dinner when Mady bit down on a crouton and said, "Mommy, my tooth hurts so bad!"

I looked in her mouth and was horrified. One of her teeth was black and rotting. I started tearing when I realized how serious this was. It must have hurt her so badly, and I didn't know how I didn't see this sooner.

Since it was Sunday evening, I couldn't do much at that point, except give her a hefty dose of Motrin and put her to bed. I arranged for a babysitter to come the next day and tried to set up a dentist appointment. Jon's new job meant we had new insurance, plus we had moved away, so we couldn't go to our old dentist. I had a recommendation for a new dentist from our pediatrician, but we hadn't seen her yet. So I left a voicemail, letting her know the situation.

The next morning the dentist's office called back and we set up an appointment for one o'clock that afternoon. Mady would have to miss school, but that was our only option. As we drove to the appointment, I had a bad feeling about it. I hated making Mady the guinea pig to meet the new dentist in this emergency situation. Mady didn't seem to mind too much. She was just chatting away. At one point, she looked out the window and saw a daycare group pushing a six-seater stroller. "Look, Mommy! They have sextuplets too. Anyway, um ..." and she continued chatting.

The dentist seemed competent enough and told us Mady had a huge cavity with an infection, but then she tried to pull Mady's tooth without Novocain. Mady was up and sitting on the chair and practically hanging from the ceiling in pain! I wouldn't have reacted any better in her situation. Drilling without pain medication? It's heartwrenching to watch your child go through something like that.

At that point, the dentist said we needed to find a pedontist, that she couldn't help us. I grabbed Mady and raced out of there.

On the way home, through her tears, Mady asked, "Mommy, why was that lady was so mean? Dr. Kristin would never do that to me." I knew what I had to do! I knew I had to do whatever I could to get her back to our old dentist.

When I got home, I called Dr. Kristin and waited to hear back from her office. I kept playing the situation over and over in my mind: Why did I l let that happen to Mady? Both Jon and I apologized to her and she just brushed it off like it was nothing. I am continually amazed by the resilience of children.

The next morning the phone rang early. Dr. Kristin's office had an opening at three that afternoon. I called Jon to make sure he could take her, and then rescheduled an eye appointment we had. This was an emergency!

Mady did really well at the dentist; she said it only hurt "like two half times and one whole time." We had no idea what that meant, but she was content and no longer in pain.

Mady at a rare trip to Dutch Wonderland.

Jon was now stuck with the fun job of wrestling with costs and insurance. He managed to pull the dentist aside, and she kindly agreed to work things out with our new insurance. I was so relieved, I started crying when Jon told me. All of our kids' dental issues would be taken care of, and we've gone to Dr. Kristin ever since. Another miracle from the Lord.

I always considered it my job to save money whenever possible, and I constantly used coupons and looked for sales. One way for me to save money was to buy in bulk or stock up during sales. That worked out well, except we were often faced with space issues. We knew an extra freezer would help so much. My surgery was what finally convinced us. I was cooking two weeks ahead in preparation for my temporary incapacitation, and I needed a place to store the food I had prepared. It was a big decision to spend $650 on an upright freezer, but the need had become urgent. We found a great sale for $550. When we came home with the freezer, my brother found a $50 coupon, so we went back and had the receipt adjusted. This thrilled me!

Another big expense for us to consider was rear air-conditioning for the Big Blue Bus. The van had front air, but because these vehicles were primarily used commercially, they weren't equipped with rear air. For us, this meant the kids in the back would roast if we traveled in hot weather. We bought battery operated clip-on fans, which did pull some of the cool air back, but it wasn't enough. For a while we attended the early service at church so we'd be home by noon or 12:30, before the heat really hit; but planning trips around the weather just wasn't practical in every situation. We knew we had to make this investment.

The solution came when we opted to drive instead of fly to Florida for our show-related trip that summer. Even though it took us nineteen hours to drive, it worked out to everyone's advantage since production picked up the cost of air-conditioning instead of

Hannah, Alexis, and Collin as we loaded up the Big Blue Bus.

ten plane tickets, and we had the lasting benefit of having rear air-conditioning in our van. This was yet another example of how the show provided for our needs that we wouldn't have been able to cover otherwise. All these perks helped us to survive.

I still see the show as a blessing that provided for many of our needs. Plus, because of the show, we pursued opportunities that we otherwise wouldn't have considered. It was important to me for our kids to be able to experience these trips because I did not have similar opportunities as a kid.

Even with the show, we couldn't have managed alone. We needed help from others. When help came, I needed to learn to accept it, which was another hard lesson for me to learn. I like to be independent.

As we settled into our neighborhood in Elizabethtown, our community reached out to us. One neighbor loved to bake and used to make us delicious cookies every other week or so — a huge neatly arranged bag of them. I so appreciated having fresh baked cookies in our house. Other people in the community used to make us dinner every so often. We didn't even know them, but their care and concern was so helpful and important to us. Someone making us dinner meant that my whole naptime was free to do laundry and catch up on other things.

While our schedule got crazier with the show, our financial pressures eased up because of increasing fringe benefits. Thankfully companies unsolicited started sending us sample product, and our kids were all too happy to open the surprise of the day. We absolutely loved it, as it helped subsidize our living costs. Then companies noticed we ate organically and sent us organic juice boxes and snacks, which was a complete luxury we certainly appreciated.

We could hardly believe how much was sent to us, as fans too would send us new and secondhand clothing and toys—stuff that we very much needed. So many of these generous people didn't want anything in return—they just wanted to help us through a difficult time where we were still living paycheck to paycheck.

I once again find myself in an uncertain financial situation now that I feel the burden of providing for eight kids and carry the weight of such a large responsibility on my shoulders.

Looking back over that time in my life when I was dependent on others to provide for our basic needs gives me the confidence to believe that no matter what, we will be taken care of. There's a verse in the Bible that talks about how God cares for even sparrows, and he takes care of us that much more. He has never let us down. I can give my worries over to God as he has shown himself faithful to us time and again.

My family weathered the season when our financial situation was a struggle, and we made it through. Our needs were always met. I know we'll get through the storm again because something, somehow will work out. It always does. Today, the mortgage is paid, food is on our table, the kids are in a school they love. I've learned to work as hard as I can while being grateful for the provisions and blessings of today, and I chose not worry about the particulars tomorrow will bring.

Letter to Hannah

Dear Hannah,

Oh sweet, sweet girl, I absolutely enjoy being your mommy! I remember the moment your name came to me. I was on the sofa in the family room of our Dauphin Avenue house, the first place you called home. I was resting and thinking of names—the two things that occupied almost every moment of my time while you were in my belly.

There was a girl in our church named Hannah. She was around my age and very sweet. I found myself thinking about her—and then her name—and I realized I loved the name Hannah … with an h on the end, of course! So when Daddy came home from work that day, I asked him what he thought about the name on my mind, and he emphatically agreed. So Hannah (or Baby B until birth) you were! Later, in keeping with Alexis's middle name, you became Hannah Joy. You have been a complete joy to raise, so your name fits you nicely.

You were born on a Monday, May 10, 2004, the day after Mother's Day. By the Friday after you were born, during one of my frequent visits to the neonatal nursery, your nurse, Sandi, asked if I would like to hold you. This was extremely exciting to me because I had not yet been able to hold any of you. So, Hannah, the nurse wrapped you in what seemed like nine million blankets and put a teeny pink hat on your doll-sized head and placed all two pounds eleven ounces of you in my anxiously outstretched arms.

I was completely unable to control the stream of tears that rolled down my cheeks as I cradled you closely for the first time since you left your spot right below my heart. I kissed you repeatedly, but your forehead was so small that each kiss nearly covered your entire face. You didn't seem to mind as you slept peacefully in your Eskimo wrap.

Every miniature part of you was exactly perfect. I almost couldn't resist the urge I felt at that moment to get up and run straight home with you in my arms—except I knew that you needed to grow and gain strength before that was possible, so you needed to stay in your protective "bubble," your incubator.

I have enjoyed watching you grow, Hannah. Almost immediately you showed maturity beyond your years. You were barely walking when you assigned yourself the task, each morning as I dressed all of you, of collecting all six pairs of pajamas and depositing them in the hamper that loomed much higher than your head. Once, when you were two and a half, you cheerily announced that you would "go downstairs and watch the kids." I laughed and thanked you as I reminded you "the kids" were the same age as you.

You have always taken pride in your independence and your ability to help me. You have always seemed to know when I have been especially tired, and it is then that you offer extra help. I don't think you know how much I have appreciated that.

Early on, you developed a love of horses, and around the same time you took pride in your long hair—your own mane! This prompted my nickname for you, "Long Hair Lilly." Sometimes you still request that I say good night to Long Hair Lilly, not Hannah! Other names you have taken on, that you have come to know and love, are "Hanni" and "Muffy." I have enjoyed seeing your gorgeous smile when I refer to you this way! It's our little thing—no one else is allowed to call you those names! So beautiful you are!

As an infant, you looked like a doll baby that I had purchased at the store. Really, you did! All of your little infant rolls were in just the right spots. You had perfectly round rosy cheeks, deep earnest brown eyes, and just the right amount of dark brown hair. As you have grown, you have taken on an exotic appearance. When you smile, the world lights up with you. Once when we visited Hawaii (remember all the fun?), a friend remarked that if we "left Hannah in Hawaii, she'd blend right in." You were too precious to leave behind, of course, so naturally we brought our little Miss Hawaii home with us.

I have enjoyed watching you grow. Even at five years old, I see who you are. You are a unique, bright, and honest little girl who is caring and loving. You are helpful and independent. You have a strong inner strength and much ability to succeed.

Over the last few years our family has changed, and this has caused pain and doubt in you. It has shaken you as it has shaken each of us. This is all expected and normal as we learn to create a new family unit and navigate these differences. I want you to know that although our family life has changed, my love for you will never ever change. I am still the "same mommy," as I frequently remind you and your brothers and sisters, and I always will be. Our structure may appear and feel different, but my goals as your mommy have not changed in any way.

I want to help you, Hannah. And I want you to learn early on a lesson that I did not learn early enough: Accept help where you need it. Make yourself humble and realize that support and care from friends and family—and sometimes people you have never met—will help you survive and succeed. Sometimes the best support comes when we least expect it from someone who we would least suspect to give it. These are angels that God sends our way to light our paths.

In return, always be vigilant, watching for others that need your help. Reach out to them, even when it's inconvenient to you, and offer your assistance. Everyone benefits from offers of help. Sometimes your help may mean the difference between existing and really living. If everyone remembered these lessons (that took me a long time to learn!), our world would be full of love and life!

I dream for you a life filled with love, a satisfying career, and family. My hope is that you learn to love God and rely on him for your needs. People will always fail you, but God never will. I assure you of this. I'll always be here for you, Hannah. I am honored to call myself your mom.

Wherever life takes you, I'll go with you helping you however I possibly can. As long as I have breath, I'll love you, support you, instruct you, and guide you every step of the way.

Love forever and always, no matter what,

Mommy

7

TOWER OF BABEL

In our house when everyone started talking, it was like the Tower of Babel—a noisy Tower of Babel. Everyone was trying to be heard, but when I couldn't understand eight out of ten words, everyone became frustrated. As twins, Mady and Cara have always been glued together and communicated with each other very well. When the little kids started talking, they tried to communicate with me, but not really between themselves, aside from Hannah and Leah.

Hannah and Leah were the first talkers and they translated as well as spoke for the group.

"Hannah, what does he want?"

"Mommy, he wants milk on his cereal."

Mady and Cara also translated for the little kids. Cara's translation was accurate; Mady's translation was what she wanted them to say. And she made it sound so good!

Collin spoke a lot, but I didn't know what language he spoke. It was always sing-songy with a lot of "mommy's" sprinkled in. Collin had a lot to say, even if I didn't understand it.

Alexis also spoke a lot, but she frequently butchered words, so we couldn't understand most of what she said. She took longer to walk or crawl when she was a baby, so she shrieked when the others came up and took her toys. For Alexis, shrieking was a tried-and-true method that she frequently fell back on. She tried so hard to be understood, but she would quickly become frustrated and then say, "Never mind." Even now she butchers words sometimes. She'll say, "What did we have for lunch, Mom? That word I can't say."

"Quesadillas."

"Oh, yeah!"

Aaden didn't talk much and Joel didn't talk at all. Hannah talked so much for Joel, in fact, that our pediatrician told me to ask her to stop.

❊ ❊ ❊

I remember one of the first conversations I had with Hannah. One day, she came into the kitchen while I was making dinner and said, "Me boo boo," while pointing to her back.

"Where's your boo boo, Hannah?"

"On my back."

"Were you jumping?"

"Yes. Jup. Mommy, I need cake." Now she was pointing to the freezer.

It took me a minute, but I finally figured out she needed the boo boo cold pack shaped like Strawberry Shortcake.

Then when she put it on her arm (close enough to her back), she said, "Mommy, I loo pity."

"You sure do look pretty," I replied as I started to heat up broccoli in the microwave.

"Mommy, my nose!"

"Your nose?" I figured she had another boo boo.

"In my nose, Mommy."

"What's in your nose, Hanni?"

"Broccies."

She smelled the broccoli!

I loved their way of communicating at this age. So simple and fun, and they were all so proud of themselves when I understood them.

Another time, when I was finishing dressing Joel and Aaden one morning, Hannah came up the stairs saying, "I need to talk to Mommy. I need to talk to Mommy." When she finally reached me in the nursery, she said, "Mommy, my jew cup [juice cup], I can't like it."

She came all the way upstairs to tell me she didn't like her juice, in her best British accent — "can't like it." Leah did like the juice, which she referred to as her "blue baby" [blueberry] juice.

Leah used to say to Jon that she likes the "hair by his mouth, hair by his nose, and hair by his ears." He loved that she said this about his beard!

This was also the time when they started telling on each other. At first, I tried to pay attention to all of it, but after so many months (now years!), I started making them deal with it themselves. Now, if someone starts a sentence with his or her brother or sister's name and unless there is bodily injury involved, I hold up my hand: "I don't want to hear it. Go work it out." Tattling is exhausting!

❄ ❄ ❄

I use their language as a way to set rules and boundaries by doing fill in the blanks. The little kids love giving the right answers. Here are some of them:

"I'm going away because I have to go to work, but I always come ..."

"Back!"

"I only go away because I ..."

"Have to!"

"Always tell the ..."
"Truff [Truth]!"
"You get what you get, and you don't get ..."
"Upset!"

❉ ❉ ❉

While the kids were using language to start communicating who they were, Jon and I used communication to survive and to handle logistics. And I think we did pretty well with that.

The good days were really good, and as a whole we worked well together. At that point our team was stronger than ever. We had the routine down, and we both knew our own responsibilities — from our schedule at home to whenever we had to go somewhere. If we were taking a family outing, I would pack everything inside and then Jon would load the food, strollers, and everything else I had packed into the van. I would dress the kids, and Jon would do the shoes and coats.

Even so, I had a lot of stress. In public I stressed about the kids running out in a parking lot — and I always wore my emotions on my sleeve. When I felt this way, it came out in anger and frustration, and I often took it out on Jon. I also didn't focus on the fact that much of the responsibility for our children, the finances, the schedules, the decisions about the future was on me, but I felt it. So I would snap at Jon.

For the first year and half at the Elizabethtown house, I was taking care of eight little kids, with little help. Normally I was by myself all day, every day — though a friend would stop by occasionally to play with the kids, my sister Kendra would come over and watch the kids while I ran out to the grocery store, and Nana Janet still came every week. But for the most part, I was by myself and exhausted, and I often felt out of control. I constantly fought the fear of a sudden injury or accident, that I would be trapped in my home and not be able to get help, or that I couldn't do things quickly or easily.

Maybe because we were often in survival mode, Jon and I didn't always communicate in a friendly manner. We had eight kids and didn't focus enough on each other. Jon once asked me, "Kate, do you realize we have been walking on eggshells for two years?" It was true. I think it was because I felt the weight of responsibility so heavily. I couldn't get sick. If I got sick, the whole camp shut down, and we didn't have time for that. A lot was riding on me, which often made me grouchy.

Even so, much of what I said to Jon was unwarranted. I could have watched what I said better, could have guarded my tongue better. And I knew it. The cameras made it obvious. So even if I didn't realize what I said at the time, it was recorded for me to watch again, and again.

I wanted to communicate better, but I often failed. I surrounded myself with 5x8 note cards with verses from the Bible about guarding your tongue: "Reckless words pierce like a sword, but the tongue of the wise brings healing" (Proverbs 12:18), and "He who guards his mouth and his tongue keeps himself from calamity" (Proverbs 21:23) I needed reminders, since I often fell back into old patterns of communicating, which weren't very pleasant. Still, I always felt love and dedication—no matter how I was communicating. No marriage is perfect, but I was committed to ours.

My communication to the outside world also needed to change. I was thoroughly annoyed with fans, with people wanting to see our kids and touch them. At the time, I considered all fan attention unwanted and an annoyance. I just didn't think through the obvious—that if I put my kids on TV people would fall in love with them. When viewers of our show would see our kids in real life, it would inevitably be exciting for them. I didn't make the connection that having people who cared—fans—meant our show continued, and therefore our job continued. I needed the fans, but I didn't know it.

I became aware of what a spoiled brat I was being. When I started speaking and telling our story and getting out in the world alone, I had the chance to look around and see reactions and responses rather than to focus so intensely on my eight kids.

When I would speak in front of an audience and tell them our story, I felt completely supported and loved by the crowd. It was truly amazing. And during my book signings, people waited in line for an autograph, and with tears in their eyes, they told me their stories in return. I've heard many times: "Kate, you're such an inspiration to me. If you can do it with eight kids, I can do it with two." That is so encouraging to me! Suddenly, I noticed a reciprocal supportive bond had formed. I now noticed that my fans had become my inspiration just as much as I was theirs. I truly am grateful for them!

I started to consciously pay attention and appreciate the people who supported me. Thousands of emails came in, crashing our server, telling us how glad they were that we were so real on TV. And I have no choice but to be real, by the way — I'm too busy to learn lines or rehearse.

I saw the world differently. I realized all moms are the same — we want the best for our families and want to do our best every day. I'm a mom first, like every other mom out there. I still identify with the unshowered stay-at-home mom wearing a dirty T-shirt and sweatpants with hair that sticks up. Being a mom can be very monotonous; stay-at-home moms need tons of encouragement as no one realizes how incredibly difficult each day is. On the other hand, it truly is the most fulfilling job you can ever have.

It wasn't until I realized this that my communication changed.

8

NO GROUP THINK

When I was pregnant with the six, I thought naively, "At least we've had twins before, so we know how to parent multiples." I couldn't have been more wrong. What you do with two, you can't do with six. My mothering had to completely change.

As every mother knows, it's important to see each child as an individual created by God. I knew that too, but with multiples, it was tempting to fall into a group mentality during their first two years. I changed all of their diapers at once, fed them the same meals at the same times, and took them to the same places together. Giving them individual treatment just wasn't doable.

When their personalities starting shining through, it wasn't possible to think of them only as a group anymore—and it started to become easier to find ways to make each child feel special for who he or she was. Their differences started to become noticeable especially when they started talking, and I could see how each of the kids is unique from any other. It is amazing to see how different each of my kids are when they all came from the same environment, same parents, same house—and are even the same age.

I began to treat them differently as they got older. I had always been strict and rigid, so it took me awhile to understand that since each child is different, we don't have to parent them the same. I needed to figure out what worked for each of them.

Other moms of multiples told us they gave certain kids permission not to nap anymore. Hearing that somehow gave me permission to parent creatively. We don't just try to be fair; we try to raise each one according to his or her own unique personalities, talents, and needs.

Sure enough, as they got older, some of the kids still needed a nap while others didn't. Cara didn't always need a nap when she was younger, so I told her to come downstairs when Mady fell asleep. Same with the little girls—Alexis always needed a nap or she'd fall asleep during dinner. Leah slept most of the time, but Hannah never did. I started telling her she could come downstairs when the other two fell asleep.

Then when Hannah and Leah started asking for a "nakin," I would let them have one at each meal. They were the only ones who did not shred or rip them. I tried to look for little things to reward each of them, so they felt like individuals.

All of the kids are so completely different that how I talk to them, discipline them, and play with them is different. With Collin I have to be firm and clear, but if I used the same voice with Aaden, he would be in tears instantly. I can treat Hannah like a seven-year-old sometimes and rationalize with her, and I can also reason with Leah; but with Alexis, I have to go over everything over and over again, since she's not as focused.

Mady and Cara have flip flopped personalities growing up; they each took turns being the dominant one. I have since learned this is

Alexis in a cozy spot.

normal for twins, though it has not been my experience in raising higher order multiples.

Alexis is silly, loves making people laugh — and trouble finds her. Hannah has always acted older and worries if anyone is sick or if things aren't fair. Aaden is thoughtful. Collin is orderly yet controlling. Leah loves girly, baby things. Joel has always been easygoing.

While I can't always give each one my undivided attention every day, each child is on my radar screen at different times. When the little girls were potty training, I didn't have to think about the boys who were still in diapers; and when I trained the boys I didn't need to focus on the girls because they had already been potty trained. It was nice to not have to worry about all of them at once. When Aaden needed glasses, he was on my radar screen. And of course, when he got glasses we needed to figure out how to keep them on his face and then to keep the other five from plucking them off his face.

With eight kids, or any number really, it's hard to have time for all of them collectively, let alone individually. I have really struggled with spending enough time with each of them. I have a lot of guilt about that, but I tried to not miss the details. My guiding principle has always been that just because I have eight doesn't mean I can't try to treat them each like an only child. I realize that's setting the bar very high, but since when do I ever set mediocre goals?

Some of the kids were more independent than others, and I just let them go. Those who wanted to hang on me more or needed more attention from me knew to come find me. I just had to trust that whoever needed the extra attention would seek it out. If someone came wandering downstairs in the middle of the night, we didn't make a big deal out of it and just scooped them up into bed with us or

Aaden with his new glasses.

made a little bed on the floor next to us. When they wanted to spend time with me in the kitchen, I put whoever came in up on the counter so we could talk while I made dinner.

When they were babies, it was harder to figure out which one needed me more; so the older they got, the easier it was to give them more attention. When Mady and Cara were old enough to start doing chores, I put together a chore chart, which included rewards. They could choose spending time alone with Mommy or Daddy, getting ice cream, or staying up an extra hour—all of which they loved. For them, time with a parent was the best reward.

Once I remember Cara really needed time alone with me, so I took her grocery shopping. At one point while we were shopping, she got a cart's length behind me and freaked out. She then asked me to call her name each time I was ready to leave the aisle. Even though she was right behind me, she was fearful I would turn the corner without her noticing, and she would once again become separated from me. Then after I loaded the groceries in the car, I returned the cart, and when I came back to the van, she was out of her seat huddled down on the ground. I was shocked that in ten seconds, she was that scared! I knew she had developed a fear that someone was going to take her or that I would lose her, but I didn't know how bad it was. I talked with her, telling her I would never put her in danger because she is my "prized possession." I told her that I loved her and would always take good care of her. I also told her that though being wary is good, she was going a little over the top. I made sure to pay extra attention to her over the next few weeks, and she seemed fine from then on.

The huge struggle with multiples or kids the same age is the classic, "It's not fair!" If I'm making a salad and give the one who's in the kitchen a crouton, they run to tell the others about it, which gets them all running in to claim their own. It's not feasible to do eight times the same thing you do for one on a whim. This reporting back to the others happened so many times that I had to tell them if they got something special in the kitchen, like a lick of icing, they weren't allowed to tell the others about it. Seems so sad, but it was necessary.

Whenever I made a cake, I dipped two additional beaters to hand out four. But because I didn't make cakes too often, it might have been another three months before I could get to the other four—and by then I wouldn't remember who hadn't yet gotten a beater. The whole situation would became a huge production, so I had to loosen the rigid rotation schedule and simply give them out to whoever was wandering through the kitchen at that time.

My motto is now "life's not fair" so hopefully they'll quit expecting me to treat them all exactly the same. Wish me luck on that!

❈ ❈ ❈

Hannah with her dinosaur egg.

I'm often asked if we gave the little kids all the same present at holidays and birthdays. We didn't. It was never economical to buy six of the same toy. They learned how to share, and they rarely all at once wanted to play with the same item.

One holiday, though, I bought each child a dinosaur egg that hatched if you put it in water for three to four days. It felt more manageable and made the kids feel special to hatch one egg at a time. When it was Hannah's turn, we were going to the beach so we had to take the stinkin' thing with us while it hatched. And we had to "guard" it wherever we were going. It was *her* dinosaur!

As a parent, it is fascinating to watch your child develop before your very eyes and bloom into a unique individual. This fact does not change when raising multiples; however, the struggles to be able to single them out and celebrate their differences does increase. During this time I started to identify what made each child tick and consciously tried to encourage each one's unique qualities. In fact, this is why I don't refer to our children as twins and sextuplets — they're individuals and this is how I view them. They each have their own needs, desires, and capabilities. Throughout life they are lumped into one group often enough by the outside world, so at home especially, they need to be encouraged to be confident in who they are as unique individuals.

Letter to Aaden

Dear Aaden,

As I sit here in the Big Blue Bus waiting for you and your brothers and sisters at the bus stop, I find myself thinking about you. You are quite an amazing little man and always have been. At a tiny 2 pounds 7.5 ounces at birth, you were the smallest of my babies. Your head was smaller than a baseball, and you had a miniscule amount of sandy blond-brown hair. You didn't have quite enough hair though to fill in the swirly of the cowlick right in the center of your hairline above your forehead. That swirly always warmed my heart and made me smile. Today, it gives you that cute little spike of hair in the front.

Although you were small, you were tough–and alert! Your incubator was on a very busy aisle. It was across from Collin and next to Hannah–although a dividing wall stood between yours and Hannah's incubators. One time I was holding you next to your busy aisle and your tiny squinty eyes followed whenever a doctor or a nurse would walk by. None of our medical team could believe how alert you were. It was so amazing to watch your little eyes following all the NICU activity.

You scared me though, Aaden! When you were two weeks old, I received a call that you were sick and that the staff caught it in time, but you slipped in your recovery. You had been doing very well and were scheduled to come home with the girls; but in the end, you and Collin came home last. The important thing is that you recovered and gained weight and were so precious! You were five pounds when you came home. Wow! Big boy!

My memories of you as a baby include you being rattled and disturbed by all of the stress and the noise in our house. You regularly cried inconsolably until you were in a dark and quiet place in the house (which was hard to find with ten family members and many helpers under one small roof) snuggled close to Mommy. Daddy would do an impression of your awareness—pursing his lips and looking around the room with your same squinty eyes. It always made us laugh!

At two, we found out you needed glasses. At first this upset me, but after you wore them for a while, I realized how extremely blessed we were that this was our only lasting effect of having six preemies—and I thanked God. You quickly grew into your new look. And the new job became keeping your glasses safely on your face. We went through many pairs and repair sessions. At over $200 a pair, it became an expensive task—but a necessary one, of course. To this day, I joke that you must think your name is "Where's your glasses?" because when you come downstairs in the morning, even after three years, you invariably forget them; and I have to remind you to go get them—to which you reply, "Oh, I get them," with your brow furrowed in your little scientific way.

As you have grown, I have enjoyed watching you develop into a quiet, thoughtful boy. You are sensitive and full of love and life. Every once in a while, something (like animals or dinosaurs) will excite you, and we see the animated, dramatic side of you—along with your brilliant smile. We all laugh with joy! It makes us want to pinch your cheeks! Your innocence is refreshing and your determination to do well is admirable.

I want you to remember an old saying, one that has guided

me in life and urged me on: "Quitters never win and winners never quit." If you always remember to finish the job, do your best, and never give up, you will succeed in life. Sometimes your best does not mean receiving a first place ribbon; but if you've done your personal best, it will translate that way in my eyes—and in yours too. Just don't quit!

Over the last months and year, our family life has changed. I want you to know that regardless of our family makeup or changes, my love for you will never change. I do not possess the skills to "father" you, but I will do everything I can to show you the way. I want to help you grow into a man of integrity—one that will be respected by others due to your undying dedication to your family, your honesty, and your determination in life. You are one of three "men" in my life, Aaden, and I appreciate the protection and help you and your brothers have already shown me and your sisters. So remarkable!

My hope is that you will have a successful career, loving family, and happiness always. I pray that as you grow, you will possess knowledge and wisdom beyond your years to help you navigate all the tricky paths that will no doubt face you. One thing is for sure: I will be next to you to answer your questions and guide you. Please come to me with anything—but especially concerns and issues that you face. Life will not be easy, but it is manageable and enjoyable if you always choose to see the bright side of life and ask advice from trusted family and friends when you need it. I love you, my oldest son, with all of my heart. This will never change!

Love forever and always, no matter what,

Mommy

9

MILESTONES

A lot of firsts occurred in the Elizabethtown house, and many of them had to do with the kids learning to be independent and growing up. Whether it was potty training or sending the girls off to school, my job was to help them take on the world outside of our home. They were learning to help around the house to contribute to the family. Sometimes the results of their independence were hilarious as they learned to do things on their own. Sometimes they were bittersweet. And sometimes they were downright right messy! While I couldn't wait for their independence and did all I could to encourage it, sometimes it was still hard to see them letting go.

From my perspective, home is a model of the world. It's the testing ground before releasing children to be on their own someday. We need to keep sight of these long-term goals, and two years old is not too early to start.

We organized the basement in such a way that all the kids could help clean up their toys. We made sure they could also follow simple instructions: Can you take this to the laundry room? Can you throw the diapers out? They also had to learn early how to respect each others' property. Their beds were their only personal space, so they were not allowed to touch anyone else's things that were in their respective beds. Their other toys were shared.

I enjoyed the milestones of them getting older. Each milestone meant one less thing we needed to do eight times. Put on your shoes and Velcro them. Put on your jacket. Make your bed. Pick up your toys. Clean up your own mess. It's not that I minded doing things for them; it's just that it was easier when they could do some themselves.

Because Mady and Cara were the big sisters, they learned to help care for the younger ones at an early age. They were helpful and kind, from helping put groceries away to handing out juice cups. They taught themselves how to read at the age of four, and now have an entire class to play with — and absolutely love being the teachers. They love to pass out spelling tests, grade them, and provide report cards.

One of the first times I started realizing our kids were growing up was when we attended the NICU reunion at the Milton S. Hersey Medical Center, which they hold every other year. I was looking forward to it. The day itself was stressful because I was supposed to work in the afternoon — though thankfully a colleague covered my first shift so I could attend. Six two-year-olds and two six-year-olds were hard enough to handle in an open public area, but we were also filming the reunion for our show, which added to the mix. It was great to see the doctors and nurses who took care of us during my pregnancy and their birth.

What I never realized before was how much joy it brings the medical staff to see the kids they took care of as tiny babies. Once babies are healthy, they leave the NICU, and those who were so important to their survival and health may never see them again. I enjoyed seeing how happy these doctors and nurses were seeing their patients again. They have a difficult, stressful job. It was very satisfying to celebrate this milestone with them and to remember how far we've come.

❊ ❊ ❊

Birthdays in our house are huge events as we celebrated their growing up together. On October 22, 2006, we threw Cara and Mady a surprise sixth birthday party. We set up a pizza parlor in the

It's a pizza (birthday) party!

garage, so the girls and their friends could make their own pizzas, and we even had a pizza cake. They were surprised and loved their party. Cara said it was better than she could have hoped for. Mady said, "Mom, you're the best!" That's the best thing a mom can hear from her growing kids.

Many may remember the little kids' third birthday carnival. It was an infamous episode on our show and was one of my favorite birthday parties to date. The games, decorations, vivid primary colors, activities (remember the pony rides?), and the guests together made for the perfect party to celebrate six perfect lives. I have always

Collin and Alexis eating cotton candy at their third birthday carnival.

felt it necessary and very warranted to host one humongous bash because after all, we were partying times six.

❋ ❋ ❋

Turning a year older meant school was just around the corner. The night before the girls' first day in kindergarten, we had their outfits picked out and had a quick shoe-tying lesson. When the girls woke up the next morning, they wanted to know "how much hours" until school. They were so excited. After lunch, Janet came over, and the girls went out to the garage to put their sneakers on. When I came out to join them a few minutes later, Cara's shoes were tied! She had tied them after only one lesson. She had grown up so much in only one day—she started kindergarten and learned to tie her shoes.

When I pulled up to the school, Cara barely hugged me and hopped out. Mady lingered a bit and hugged long before running off.

When it was time for them to come home, Janet helped get the six up from their nap, and we all hustled out to the porch to see the girls get off the yellow bus. They were all excited to see their big sisters on their big day. I taped the bus coming into the neighborhood and ran to the stop to see them getting off. I snapped pictures and kept saying, "You only get this chance once!" I'm sure the other moms all thought I was nuts.

When Jon came home, the girls got a kick out of him saying,

"Hello, my kindergarteners." The girls loved school and were so proud to be "big school kids."

❊ ❊ ❊

The girls starting school meant potty training for the little kids. Potty training is one of the more challenging aspects for parents. My mantra has always been that if I'm changing a diaper and their toes hit my nose, they need to be potty trained. It's plain ridiculous to be inadvertently kicked in the face when changing diapers.

When the little girls were ready, I started potty training them before worrying about the boys. This is already a messy time between accidents and purposely pouring the potties on the floor, that I didn't need to keep track of six at a time. Three was enough.

When one of the girls pooped in the potty, I took a picture of her next to the potty so she could show Daddy when he got home. After about a month the three girls started wearing big girl underwear — or "unna wears," as Leah called them.

One Sunday in the middle of potty training, we picked up the kids after church, and the teacher was telling me that Hannah pooped

Little Leah "reading" a magazine on the potty.

in her Pull-Up and that he changed her. I couldn't hear him over the hallway commotion. As we were all walking down the hall together, Hannah said, "Mommy, I told Jesus that I had to go potty." Jon and I both laughed hard.

Later in the car we started laughing again about it, and Jon asked, "Hannah, what is your teacher's name?"

She replied, "Jesus."

Mystery solved.

Then came the boys, which definitely did not go as smoothly. They were always more focused on playing in the moment than on planning for the future. I am always amazed that the girls were potty trained a full six months before the boys. Even so, they were all growing up, regardless of whether or not they chose to be potty trained.

❀ ❀ ❀

One Sunday, I was sitting on the sofa in the playroom with everybody. Hannah climbed up next to me, and I asked her if she would sit on my lap.

She said, "No, I wanna sit."

"But you are my baby, and I want to hold you."

"I not a baby. I girl."

I almost cried. These are the youngest kids I'll ever have. They are two, and they sometimes don't want to sit on my lap anymore. But I suppose this is all a part of the mixed emotions I'll experience at each of their milestones.

10

BLOOD, BAND-AIDS, AND BATHS IN THE KITCHEN SINK

One phone call, one sick child, one exhausted mom. Any one of these could throw off an otherwise good day. While at the time I couldn't always laugh in the moment, I've learned the importance of keeping a healthy perspective and remembering to laugh later. One of my most memorable bad days happened one summer in 2006.

In July our church had a Vacation Bible School (VBS) program in the evenings for a week. Jon had to come home from work early, and the plan was that I would have the kids ready to go so we could all just hop into the van to make it to church on time. While the little kids were taking a nap on that Monday afternoon, I was making dinner and getting ready to go that night. When it was time to get them from their nap, I headed upstairs and opened their bedroom door.

"OH! OH MY!" There were shards of glass everywhere, and the

The aftermath of the nursery destruction.

kids were walking all around them. For a split second, I thought a burglar had broken in, but I quickly realized they had gotten into a locked bin that held diapers and lotions, and had smeared butt paste all over the room. "Let me check your feet," I frantically said. The broken glass around the room was my main concern.

I picked each kid up and brought them one by one to the bathroom to clean them up. But what was that sticky stuff everywhere? "Where are your diapers? Is that poop on—?"

As if getting into the clean diapers wasn't enough, they had ripped off their own diapers, along with the accompanying poop.

Breathe, Kate, breathe, I had to remind myself.

With the kids finally cleaned up and a fresh diaper on each one, I left them in the bathroom while I ran down to my bedroom to grab the camera. When I walked back into the war zone—their bedroom—I surveyed the damage and took photos. I still couldn't believe it: Dressers were knocked over with drawers spilling out their contents. Light bulbs and lamps were broken, which is where the glass came from. It was nothing short of a miracle that no one was hurt or cut.

Why hadn't I heard anything? I had been downstairs the entire time! How could this have happened without me knowing?

"Is that a hole in the wall?" I realized they had even peeled a section of paint and drywall off the wall. I started to freak out, but consoled myself by remembering that no one was hurt or trapped under the dresser. This could have been disastrous.

I knew we really should have been downstairs eating dinner already in order to be ready by the time Jon got home, but this was going to take hours to clean. Exhausted and overwhelmed, I called my dear friend. "Carla, you're not going to believe this ..." Carla has rescued me more times than I can count and offered to come over to help.

I picked my way over to the dressers and pulled out clothes for church and shut the door on my way out. I didn't see the room in that shape again. Carla and her husband cleaned the entire room by the time we got home, and it was as good as new — with only the patch of missing drywall to remind me.

Notice the missing drywall.

❊ ❊ ❊

One night, when the little kids were two and a half, we were all upstairs in the nursery playing before bed. I was exhausted as usual and was laying on the floor while they were playing on top of me. The girls would play with my hair while the boys drove their trucks on my back and arms and legs, like I was a highway — a toddler massage. Hannah came over with a heavy plastic piggy bank and dropped it on the corner of my eye and eyebrow. I felt pain shoot through me as I gripped my head.

Blood was everywhere, and I thought I needed stitches. I figured we couldn't go to the hospital. Who would we get to watch the kids so Jon could take me? The cut ended up not being as bad as I thought, so I just put pressure on it and then a pressure bandage. I was okay, though I have a nice scar. Hannah felt sad that she gave me an accidental "boo boo" and offered me "cake."

Between injuries and bloody noses, I have to do some kind of first aid or get out the Band-Aids every single day. Blood and injuries no longer cause panic. They are as normal as mealtime!

Another time after we put the little kids to bed, Jon and I were in the garage opening and organizing fan mail and packages. Cara and Mady came down and said someone was crying. We asked if they could go see what was wrong; but after ten minutes went by, they didn't come back to tell us what happened. So we went upstairs to check it out, thinking the girls just settled whoever it was back to sleep.

They were near Leah's toddler bed, trying to calm her. I don't know why they didn't come back and tell us what was wrong. When I asked them, they said, "Mommy, we felt something wet on her forehead when we were putting her back into bed, and thought it was just tears." We figured Leah had thrown up so Jon grabbed a flashlight and went in to investigate. He quickly realized it was blood, so he grabbed Leah while I went in and started cleaning up.

The blood was everywhere! I thought she had had a bloody nose, until Jon realized when he was bathing her that Leah had a huge gash on her forehead! It was about a half inch long, and while not deep, it was gaping open. I put a pressure bandage on it, gave her Tylenol for the pain, and let her sleep in our room that night so we could keep an eye on it.

In the morning, the wound was still weeping blood a little bit, so I called a neighbor who was an emergency room nurse to come over and take a look. I didn't want to subject Leah to stitches on her head unless it was absolutely necessary as it would cause her more pain and agony. My neighbor said Leah could probably use a stitch, she wasn't sure, so she got some Steri-Strips and we bandaged her together. We kept the wound clean and covered it in antibiotic cream.

I still don't know what happened to Leah, and that left me a bit

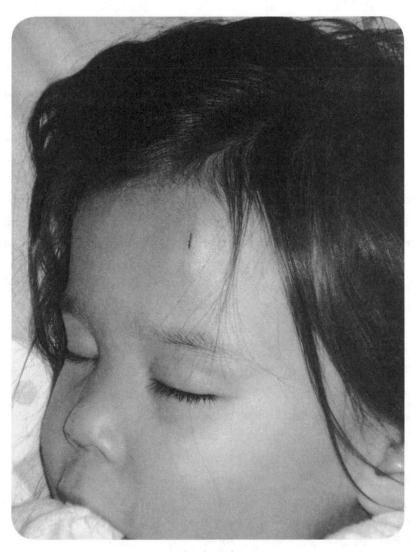

Leah's boo boo.

unsettled. But God knew exactly what happened, and I knew he loved Leah more than we did—which was mind-boggling, because I love her a lot. I prayed that he would protect her little head and help it to heal without a scar and without infection. Mostly I was thankful he did not let something worse to happen to her. She healed beautifully.

❀ ❀ ❀

During the first winter in the Elizabethtown house, the flu was going around in our family. One afternoon all the kids were settled into their beds for a nap, and Jon was out doing errands with Cara and Mady. Alexis, who was the last one to get the flu, was resting in a makeshift bed on the floor of our bedroom while I was at the computer. Sitting with my back toward her, I began to hear alarming sounds. I turned to see her attempting to cry with each cry being interrupted by a strange jerking movement. Each lurch would cause her to cry louder and harder. As I rushed to her side, I saw fear in her eyes. After feeling her burning hot forehead, I realized she was having a febrile seizure—something I had walked through with parents many times on the phone when I worked as a nurse in the pediatric office.

I had no idea these could be so scary, and I fought to keep my emotions at bay. It didn't work though, as my mother-mode quickly overtook my nurse-mode. I frantically tried to call Jon back home, and when I couldn't reach him, I then called a friend who wasn't available. When panic took over completely, I ended up calling 9-1-1. I knew there was nothing they could do—I could only put her in a lukewarm bath to get her fever down—but I needed reassurance that I was doing everything I could do. Alexis was limp between her intermittent jerking as I sat on the floor rocking her. When I saw the whites of her eyes as they were rolling back into her head, I was completely terrified and started sobbing.

In the end, I was able to cool Alexis down gradually in the bathtub so her seizure stopped, and I knew it was now safe to give her Motrin to help ensure that her temperature would return to normal. She was much better by the time the emergency crew arrived and Jon got home. This truly was one of the scariest times I've experienced as a mom.

I recall another health concern when Hannah started getting headaches when she was two. Every so often she would come down the stairs in the morning complaining of a stomachache and headache. At first I didn't know what was really happening, but when her headaches persisted, I took her to the pediatrician, who ordered a CAT scan and confirmed Hannah was having migraines. The doctor explained that a migraine could be triggered by getting woken up too early. Hannah has always slept in later than Alexis and Leah, and they would often wake her up in the morning, which sometimes triggered the migraines. When the migraines came, we figured out a routine: I would give her Tylenol, which she promptly threw up; she would then fall asleep for an hour or two and wake up completely better.

Her headaches continue every so often but at least now I know what to do.

❄ ❄ ❄

I have to confess that I didn't handle all this chaos well all the time. One infamous Friday in October, we started out with the usual stuff: diaper changes, breakfast, playtime in the basement, and lunch. Then I put the little kids in their cribs for naps, got the girls off to school, cleaned up, and ate my own lunch while watching a cooking show on TV. The awful part came after the nap.

I went up to get the little kids at 3:30 as usual. Hannah and Leah were still sleeping so I let them sleep while I got the other four and we went downstairs to wait for the school bus. The girls were still asleep when I went back up at 4:30, but I decided to wake them up anyway. I went over to Leah and I couldn't believe my eyes! She was asleep with poop from head to toe and all over her crib! Poop was mashed into the bottoms of both feet and on her sheet, blankets, a book in her crib — some was even flung to the edge of Alexis' crib.

I was so mad and woke her up with my angry voice. I put her in the bathtub and stood her in an inch of water to soak her feet and showered her. Poor little Leah was shaking, as I cleaned her up. Then I had to clean up her crib. All this happened after the other four had gotten into the tissue box on Grandma's desk (again!), and Alexis had gotten into the baby wipes in the bathroom and was trying to flush them down the toilet, which was completely clogged at this point.

As soon as I had Leah's mess cleaned up, I realized I didn't know where Alexis was, again. When I called her, she came running into the room, soaking wet. She had made a pool of water on the kitchen floor with the waterspout from the freezer door. I seriously lost it, so I put her in her crib until Jon got home and told him he could get the "monster" and feed her dinner. I was so frustrated! Of course she's not a monster, but she was surely capable of monster messes and I didn't know what to do at that point.

I felt so guilty about how I handled everything. After everyone was in bed, I journaled about the events and prayed for patience — again. It was late and I didn't know quite how cheery I would be in the morning when I greeted them, but I knew all their smiling faces would help. And of course, their "Hi Mommy" voices would make me melt. Thank goodness for their grace!

Every mom knows what it's like when something unexpected interrupts her day. But with eight kids under six years old, a single event could change my day from calm to chaotic. With two six-year-olds and six two-year-olds in one house, one event would trigger seven others until the neatly stacked dominoes of the day toppled into a heap.

Wednesday, February 28, 2007, was yet another one of those days. Although it wasn't funny at the time, I can now laugh about the series of events that took place that afternoon.

The morning went smoothly, and I was feeling quite accomplished. After lunch, the older girls went off to school and the little kids went down for a nap. For weeks, I had been waiting for a conference call with the Discovery Health Channel, the executives in charge of our show. It was scheduled for that afternoon.

Promptly at two o'clock, I called the number I had been given. Each of the participants on the call introduced themselves, and we'd just gotten into the heart of the discussion when the phone beeped. I glanced at the caller ID and saw it was the girls' school on the other line. It was 2:17, and there wasn't a good reason for them to be calling me unless there was trouble.

"Excuse me, but my daughters' school is calling and I need to take this call. I'll be right back." I switched to the other line.

"Hello?"

"Hi, Kate. This is Mady's teacher. I'm sorry to bother you, but Mady has a bloody nose."

I could hear Mady crying hysterically in the background.

"She's really upset and she wants to come home. Do you want to talk to her?"

"Yes, please put her on."

The sound of Mady's crying intensified as she got closer to the phone. "Mady, Mady, calm down. Are you okay? Tell me what happened." She was crying so hard I couldn't understand what she was trying to say. I quickly realized I couldn't do anything over the phone. "Listen, Mady, I will come and get you just as soon as I can find someone to sit with the little kids. Please calm down. I am coming to get you."

The Discovery Health executives would have to understand. I

clicked back to the conference call. "I'm sorry but I am going to have to reschedule this meeting." I hung up before they had a chance to reply and frantically dialed neighbors to get someone to stay with the six. For normal families, it would be as simple as putting a kid or two in a car seat to make a quick run to the elementary school. But for me, it meant waking six kids from a nap, changing six diapers, and trying to buckle six crying babies into six car seats by myself. It just wasn't practical. After a few calls, my sister-in-law was available. Thank goodness!

While I waited for her to get there, I went to the bathroom to comb my hair. I wasn't one of those people who had to get dolled up just to leave the house; at that time I often left without any makeup. Getting pretty took time I just didn't have then. But when I looked in the mirror that afternoon, my appearance scared even me. I jumped into the shower and did a ten second rinse off. I barely dried off and got dressed while I was still wet.

When my sister-in-law arrived, I rattled off instructions while grabbing the keys and heading to the door. My imagination got the worst of me on the ride to school. What condition would Mady be in when I got there?

As I ran into the school building, the sight of Mady surprised me. She was sitting in the office smiling and apparently happy. I think the whole commotion embarrassed her. I felt so bad for her. I hugged her, signed her out, and took her home.

By the time I got home, the little kids were already stirring. My sister-in-law slipped out, and I left the kids in their beds a few minutes longer while I got Mady settled. Fortunately, her nose had stopped bleeding. I just needed to clean her up.

After I got the little kids up and changed their diapers, I did something I rarely did—I offered them a snack. It was already four o'clock. Usually, dinner was cooking before then, but in all the excitement, I hadn't even started preparations. While they ate, I washed the chicken breasts and started broiling them in the oven. I filled a large pot with water for the pasta and started grabbing the ingredients I would need. I made trip after trip to the pantry as I consulted the recipe. I think there were about nine hundred ingredients on the counter by the time I finished.

On one of these trips, I heard Leah say her belly hurt, but I didn't pay much attention. I concentrated on finishing my already-late dinner, and I was only half listening. But when I heard a choking sound, I stopped what I was doing and looked down to see Leah lying on the shag rug in front of the kitchen sink, inches from my feet. She was vomiting. Not once, not twice, but what seemed to be a continuous stream. I ran over to her and sat her up so she wouldn't choke. I tried to hold her over the rug so that the liquid, if not the smell, would be at least somewhat contained.

When Leah finished, I stood to rinse out the sink. (When we moved into that house, I had the old sink taken out and an industrial sized sink put in; I called it the tub because it was larger than anything you would normally see in a residential kitchen.) I scrubbed that sink, then filled it with clean water. I lifted Leah to the counter and carefully peeled off her vomit-drenched clothing and put her in the "tub" to clean her up.

I sent Hannah to get a bucket. Cara went to get a towel. And Mady and Alexis got a clean outfit for Leah. Later, I chuckled. I knew that I must have been desperate to send those two girls together as they were not the combination to get anything in an emergency. But I didn't have a choice.

While naked Leah sat splashing in the sink, I turned the nearly blackened chicken and made sure the noodles didn't overcook. Leah had a blast playing while I alternated between washing her and continuing the dinner preparations.

Once my sweet girl was bathed, I handed her off to Cara and Mady who dressed her in a lovely combo of clothes chosen by her

Leah splashing away in her sink bath.

sisters. Of course the clothes didn't match, but I didn't care because at least she was dressed.

I piled the vomit-filled rug and clothes into the cherry red bucket and remembered to set the oven timer before I headed to the laundry room. Once I got everything in the washer, I returned to the kitchen.

The kitchen was a mess. Ingredients were strewn everywhere, pots were boiling over, and the floor was a slippery skating rink of fluids from Leah's body. I had no choice but to tackle the mess before me, so I did. Fortunately, an earlier SOS call I had placed to Jon was rewarded with his timely return from work, and we were all able to eat dinner together. And you know what? The dinner wasn't even burned. It was actually delicious!

I'm a person who likes things orderly and in control, and that afternoon greatly tested me, but this time I passed. I came to see that life may never be as tidy as I dream of it, but I can adapt—most times, anyway.

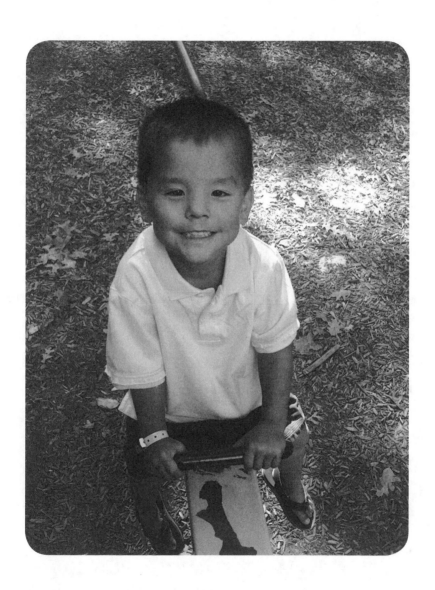

Letter to Collin

Dear Collin,

   The story of your name is not a mystery for sure. I know that by now you have heard a million times how Mady chose your name. She was just three years old and wanted a baby brother. She asked repeatedly and even declared your name would be "Collin." So, naturally, when Daddy and I learned the news that we would be having seven (which later became six), we knew that you would be Collin—although you spent the entire time in my belly being referred to as "baby F." You were located on the bottom right side in a tiny spot, with Joel sitting on top of you the entire time you were in my belly. I laugh now because I wonder if that is the reason you and Joel tend to annoy each other at times. You had already spent a lot of time in close quarters together by the time you were born.

   At birth, you were the biggest baby—the only one who broke three pounds. And don't forget the half ounce above. Every little bit counted at that size! You were my big boy. Even though you were big, you actually struggled a lot. Due to your respiratory issues, I was not able to see your face for two weeks following your birth. It really bothered me that I didn't know what my little boy looked like. And furthermore, I couldn't even hold you! I remember the first time Daddy and I were able to hold you. We left Cara and Mady to swim with friends on that Sunday afternoon and drove to the hospital eagerly. We held you for a short time before you started to have difficulty breathing. But it was so good to see who you were—even if it was cut short. You had gorgeous dark brown eyes and floppy cheeks that were precious. I loved holding you close!

I have enjoyed watching you grow and remember the first time I knew you were a genius. You were barely two and I was changing your diaper and dressing you. You said, "Boo, Mommy." I thought you were trying to scare me until I realized you were pointing at your blue shirt. I had no idea you knew your colors, but when I started pointing to every different color in the room, you proved it to me. I was quite astonished! And my amazement of your intelligence didn't stop there. You are the only five-year-old I know who can add 17 and 21 (far from the only addition problem you can do mentally) and come up with the correct answer!

You, by nature, are also very sweet, kind, and helpful. I encourage you to continue to use these gifts and help others whenever you can. I have seen you help your brothers and sisters as well as myself, and it warms my heart. Keep it up, sweet boy. We appreciate you!

As you have grown, however, I must say you have also challenged my authority greatly. At two and a half, you began testing and trying my parenting at every chance. I called Daddy at work many days crying because you would not obey. I had to ask you every day, "Who's in charge: you or me?" You would reluctantly answer, "You are." As you have grown, this fact has not changed. You continue to be determined to do what you want to do, and I continue to try to rein you in.

Most days, I am able to see that this determination is a quality I also possess. It is a quality that will take you far—as long as you make the right choices in life. This determination will not allow bumps in the road or tall mountains placed in your path to deter you. You will prevail and succeed at whatever you attempt. This perseverance is a wonderful quality if steered correctly. I am working on good choice versus bad choice with you now at five years old. I pray that your good choices in life will far outweigh your bad choices. If you allow me, I will be with you, helping you to make the right choices so that you are able to succeed always.

Although I obviously do not possess the skills necessary to father you, I will walk with you and help guide you as I do my very best to mother you. I desire for you a rewarding career, a healthy, loving family, and happiness always. I pray that you will grow to love God and make choices that please him always.

I know that the recent events in our family structure have greatly upset you—maybe you most of all. I want you to know that I have made and will continue to make decisions based on what I believe is best for you and your brothers and sisters. These changes, I realize, are still painful and hurt a lot. I want you to know that my love for you will never change. I will never leave you; and when I must leave to go to work, I will always come back. I will always be your "same mommy," as I often remind you now. You and your brothers and sisters are the reason I breathe. That fact will never change.

Thank you, Collin, for the complete honor of being your mommy! There is a special place in my heart that has your name on it.

Love forever and always, no matter what,

Mommy

11

I AM MOM, HEAR ME ROAR

As moms, we are defined by the most important job we do — taking care of our kids. Being a mother is the most tiring job you will ever have, and it's the most worthwhile job. And while we are busy creating the memories and traditions that will provide our kids with a good foundation, for some reason, everyone has an opinion of how we should look or act as a mom. Add in the issue of whether a mom needs to stay at home or work outside of the house, and we have a whole new set of pressures, beginning with the pressure and guilt we put on ourselves.

There are days I just don't do a good job as a mom and I know it. Every mom gets exhausted, frustrated, and feels guilty, and I often felt this way with so many toddlers. Frequently in my journal I wrote the words, "I was less than patient with the kids today. Sometimes I am so tired that my fuse is almost nonexistent. It's not fair for the kids to have an impatient mom. Tomorrow I will do a better job."

And I often prayed for patience, as this prayer illustrates:

Lord, thank you for loving me no matter what kind of mom I've been today. Thanks for being a perfect role model for me as a parent. Thank you, Lord, for each one of my amazing children. Thank you for all of their dear little faces and for the daily chaos they provide our house with. Please help me to see all the noise and chaos and irritations as good things—because they are all healthy enough to cause these things. Thank you for choosing to give each of them to me. Help me to be a patient and loving mother and not a mean and yelling crazy mother! Please remind me when I get out of line that I need to be more patient. Thank you, Lord, for a fresh new start tomorrow to do better. Amen.

Our kids needs always come first, but we should not be paralyzed by mommy guilt when we aren't perfect. I feel guilt when there's not enough time for each kid individually. I had eight young kids, and I needed to keep the house running—bills paid, meals cooked, laundry done, house cleaned, appointments scheduled, etc. I didn't have a lot of time for each of them individually each day.

I felt guilt when I was too tired to play a game with them in the evenings. By the end of the day, I was just exhausted and didn't always have the energy to run outside and play with them. I sat a lot in the evenings, as I had run around all day taking care of them. By the time seven p.m. came I was ready for bed. I was so grateful Jon would come home and play with them in the backyard. I was out there with them, but often I wasn't actively playing.

I felt guilt when I couldn't hear them over each other's noise when someone was trying to tell me something important.

I felt guilt when I'd spoken too harshly with a child and could have responded better. It's particularly a struggle to figure out the right way to handle a child when they have hurt their brother or sister on purpose. When I was lying in bed reviewing the day, I would think of all the things I could have done differently.

I felt guilt when we didn't have money for special things for each of them. We took them to the playground quite a bit, but we couldn't afford Hershey Park, which was local. Every so often we took them for ice cream, but even that got expensive with eight kids. We just wanted to give them as normal of a childhood as possible. I thank God we were able to afford some of these things when we were filming the show, but even then there just wasn't extra money for eight kids and everything you want to give them.

I see being a mom as the best yet hardest job in the world. It's so hard to live up to the high standards we place on ourselves, and I'm trying to learn that we just have to do our best as moms. No one is perfect; everyone makes mistakes. We need to let go of our mommy guilt, get up tomorrow, and do a better job. Tomorrow is a new day, which promises a fresh start. As long as we're doing our best every day, keeping our kids safe and healthy, showing our hearts to our kids so they know we love them, that's all that matters. Mommy guilt is harmful and paralyzing, not helpful. I've come to realize that the kids I have are the exact kids God gave me; and for whatever reason, he thought I could do a good job parenting them. I am giving it my very best shot!

It's not only the pressure we put on ourselves that causes guilt. It feels to me like moms often criticize other moms, especially when it comes to our appearance. This one is hard for me since my mommy transformation has played out so publically. Is there a law that says that once you have kids, you have to look frumpy and wear mom jeans and have mom hair? Didn't we take care of ourselves before we had kids?

It's important not to lose track of who you are. Besides, I think looking nice sets a good example for our kids. I've found that it improves self-confidence, which we can then pass along.

I went through my years of living in sweatpants and a T-shirt tie-dyed with food and snot. Sometimes I didn't have time to shower for three days or woke up in the morning wearing the same thing I wore the day before (and I can guarantee it wasn't clean). I had my hair cut short since I didn't have time to care for it long anymore. I wanted to be able to wake up in the morning and have my hair look the same,

whether or not I brushed it. It was easy, quick, manageable.

But as my kids started to get older and needed less around-the-clock care, I tried to use our treadmill every day when they were asleep. I found it to be a great stress reliever.

One of the things I did for myself while I was recovering from my surgery was to get my hair cut and colored back to blonde. At the end of that day — with me in a new body, a new outfit, and a new hairstyle — the girls at the salon said they couldn't believe my change from even a week earlier. One stylist said I looked like a model, which was fun to hear, even though I knew I still looked like a mom — though maybe an improved mom. I mention this comment because it meant so much to me at the time that I wrote it down in my journal. As moms, we don't get all the encouragement we need, and I hope my stories give hope to other mothers who feel the same way. It's okay to take care of yourself and feel beautiful!

I do feel a little self-conscious about this topic, because I did have the amazing opportunity to have a tummy tuck, and not everyone gets that chance. But even if I hadn't, I would still feel it's important to emphasize and be an example to my daughters the importance of taking care of yourself. You don't have to be perfect, but it is important to be healthy and to feel good about yourself.

When my kids were little, I couldn't spend much time on looking good. Dressing up consisted of putting on jeans to wear to the store, donning scrubs for work on Saturdays, and trying to look decent for church. I didn't have time to care about what I wore outside of those occasions. In April 2008 I did my first promotional campaign, and started feeling somewhat like a professional. Transitioning to a new career gave me the excuse to fix myself up. I bought a few jackets for meetings and carried a work bag.

I hated being away from the kids though. The first time I left for a business trip to New York on my own, I got in the car and said to the driver, "You better go quick, or else I'm getting out." I didn't want to do it alone—without Jon or my family—but the income really made a difference for us.

In tears, I once asked my friend how he traveled for work, leaving his family at home, and he said, "I know they are at home and are okay so I try to focus on work and get home as soon as possible."

I couldn't help but think, "Easy for you to say. You're the dad. You're supposed to do this kind of thing; that's normal."

Being from a conservative suburban area, I struggled with gender stereotypes. Whenever Jon and I met a couple, I seemed to relate better to the husband than the wife. The husband was usually a type-A personality, and he usually handled the finances—which is what I did. And that bothered me. I wanted to be a typical wife, as I understood it. I eventually learned to accept that whoever was best suited for each task should do it, and not consider it a gender issue—but it took awhile. My angst and stress left as I learned to accept who I am.

145

This identity confusion also translated into career questions. In our circle, moms usually stayed home while dads went to work, so sometimes it was difficult for the kids to understand why I was not home. Again, that came down to who was better suited for the task. Jon didn't want to travel and speak—he did it, but he didn't enjoy it—so he gave me his blessing to go ahead. I loved it, but I had to get over this guilty feeling of leaving my kids.

The good thing about our parenting styles was that we were equally involved, so the kids responded to both parents the same. One parent was as good as the other in our house. The kids got to the point where they wouldn't blink when I would leave on trips. Dad was there, and they still had their stability. They were used to their schedule and Jon followed it exactly. They were always happy to see me when I came home, but they didn't hang on my legs when I left. Also, Jon was involved in what I was doing outside the home too, as I discussed everything with him before I accepted any engagements.

In New York City, I noticed other moms were on the job scene as well. Where I lived, the career mom was not normal, but in New York it was. It was good to fit in. I missed my kids, but I realized many other moms did as well. I learned to talk to my kids on the phone and love them from afar, reminding myself that I had to do my job.

I didn't know I would enjoy business, but after taking it on as a new challenge, I realized I loved it. Nursing had never been my ideal career, though it prepared me to be a better mom to my kids because I don't have to rush them to the doctor every five seconds—part of God's unique design for me, for which I am grateful. The challenge of this new career fit me perfectly, and I wanted to do more. I truly enjoyed the campaigns, books, shows, media—and people! I hadn't always been good with people, being isolated in the house for the larger part of seven years, so it was a pleasant surprise to find how much I liked it.

I've come to realize that moms come in different packages — the stay-at-home mom, the working mom, the single mom.

When I started working and traveling, I couldn't help but wonder if I was still a real mom. "Someone else is taking care of my kids right now, someone else is making their dinner, someone else is checking their homework." Even if that someone else was Jon, I still had to remind myself that I was a real mom who needed to provide for my kids, and just because that provision now took on a different appearance didn't mean I was any less of a mother.

Looking back, I feel fortunate that I signed up for those campaigns as they were good steps to building a career. I can see how God was preparing me for this time in my life; being a single mom, I now have to work to provide for my kids. Imagine if I never took on those other opportunities and remained a stay-at-home mom. My kids would have had to adjust to another change when I was thrust into the workforce. But they're used to it now — and very proud of their hard-working mom!

I'm glad we were able to get used to the traveling piece of my job during that simpler time, because no matter what, it's not easy. When I first began traveling, they missed me, but Jon was with them and kept to a strict schedule, so everything was the same. After a while, when I would go to leave, they would simply say, "Bye, Mommy," since they were with their dad. It hurt my feelings a bit since they didn't seem to mind my leaving, but it was good they were comfortable. Now they hang on me and say, "Please don't go, Mommy. When will you be back?" They no longer have that stability.

It's hard, but we work around it. When I'm traveling, they can call me anytime. Whenever my phone quacks — my ringtone for home — I dive on it. Cara calls me in the morning before she leaves for school. I need to be available to them even when I'm not there in person, to have a presence even in my absence. I often say — and people close to me know — I not only run my home when I'm there, but I'm always at home in my heart — even if I'm far away.

Letter to Leah

Dear Leah,

Oh my little dainty princess! What a lovely addition you are to our family, tiny though you are. At birth, you were actually the largest girl, second in size only to Collin. It's amazing to think now how you could have been 2 pounds 14.8 ounces and end up my teeniest child. In our world of preemies, almost three pounds was like ten pounds.

You sailed through your time in the neonatal unit—without an issue or a problem as you spent your days next to the large window with a view identical to mine from the ten weeks prior. Had you been aware enough, you could have watched the deer family I observed regularly through the window on that side of the hospital. Their antics occupied my many spare hours while you steadily grew in my belly.

You were exquisite (as Great Grandma always said) and perfect in every way from day one. You had a lot of dark brown hair on your head—and on your arms and back! Your cheeks were rosy and you were so very precious.

The story of your name is an interesting one. I had always wanted a "Morgan" since I had babysat for many years and loved a little girl by this name. Daddy and I both loved the name and thought that was settled. But as time passed, I realized I didn't want to confuse things by giving gender-neutral names, so I began to rethink it. I remembered a little

Korean girl in Great Grandma's church by the name of Leah, and she was beyond precious. She was always happy and giggling, which caused me to not only love her but also her name! So Leah you were.

In keeping with Alexis's and Hannah's middle names, we decided to call you Leah Hope. Our prayers gave us much hope that all six of you would be born alive and healthy. As you know now, Leah, that prayer has been answered completely!

I count your health and the health of your brothers and sisters as my biggest blessing—especially on rough days, when the bickering is overwhelming and being a single mommy of eight kids begins to feel like too much. I try to always see the positive in everything, which allows me to step back and be grateful that you are "able" to bicker and fight—even when you come zooming into the kitchen to tattle for the nine hundredth time in an hour, Leah!

Although cute, you were a difficult baby—not in temperament but in feeding. You had reflux, which caused you to vomit nearly every drop of every feeding. It became a challenge to avoid jostling you so that you wouldn't "lose your lunch," literally. Nanny Joan, as you know, lovingly fed you daily and sat among the many drop cloths that covered the sofa, often wearing the contents of your bottle no matter how careful she was. She happily made it her self-assigned task to see to it that you kept your food where it belonged. She loves you so much, Leah! I appreciated Nanny Joan's help much more than I remembered to tell her. But I know that some of your first smiles flashed in her direction were surely thanks enough for her.

It became apparent to me that Nanny Joan knew almost better than I how to feed you, and it made me sad. It was difficult for Mommy to miss out on so many feedings and snuggles with each of you, but I had to allow others to help and fill in the gaps where I wasn't enough. I remember wanting to pluck all six of you from the arms of your feeders and run. Just because I had six babies didn't mean that I didn't love each of you as if you were my one and only. In fact, I struggled constantly with the guilt I felt because I had to divide myself—and still do—in so many ways.

Over time, as I've learned to be a more positive thinker, I've come to realize that the love and the support of close family and friends was important and good for you—and a close second to my mommy love.

As you grew that first year, you easily overcame the reflux and developed completely normally. Whew! I've often wondered if your rough start caused you to drop from my biggest girl to my tiny princess, as I call you.

You were my first and most enunciated talker. I also give Nanny Joan the credit for that, as she told you volumes day after day as you both sat still as statues in that drape covered throne … I mean, chair. You were so little, but crystal clear when voicing your requests, concerns, complaints, and desires—and everyone else's issues for that matter. Many times I have just cracked up at your mature and unexpected responses! Just today I asked you a question, and your answer was a very poised, "Why yes, I do!" As usual, I had to chuckle at the uniqueness of you!

As you have grown, I have enjoyed your contribution to our family. You add an excitement that only you can add. You are pleasant and kind and helpful. I admire the fact that you interact and love each of your brothers and sisters equally.

Please always remember what I tell you often at the dinner table: "Look around you. These are your best friends. They will be

151

by your side helping you long after I am gone. Other friends will come and go, but these are your true friends." These are important words to remember. Please always strive to remain close to your family. It may be difficult at times, but don't ever allow anything to entice you to become disloyal to those who are closest to you. The perceived benefit of friends will never outweigh the bond you have with family. Strong bonds with trustworthy allies will help you survive in a world where loyalty is cashed in regularly to get ahead in life. Always remain dedicated to those who have proven their loyalty. I promise you, it will be worth the struggle.

Recently our family life has changed. I know that you have wrestled with these changes. It is evident to me that you are sad; and when you are sad, I am sad. I just want you to know that I am here for you and that my love for you will never change. I will be your "same mommy" for all of time. Nothing and no one will ever take your place in my heart.

You recently told me, "I've waited my entire life" for something on your Christmas list; just the same, I've waited my entire life to be your mommy. I want to walk beside you, holding your hand as you grow and learn to navigate the sometimes scary, sometimes happy, and sometimes difficult times ahead of you. I dream for you a successful career, a happy marriage, and a fulfilling family life. Come to me when you need a hug, a hand, or just your mommy with a heart that swells with love for you—today, tomorrow, and forever. I'm here for you!

Love forever and always, no matter what,

Mommy

12

PLAYING SAFE

After the show started airing, our privacy disappeared. People would run up on our porch and take pictures through our windows, park in front of our house to watch our kids ride their bikes, park on the side of our house to watch them play in the backyard. We couldn't do anything to stop it. We were on display like fish in an aquarium. Our house was also close to the road without fencing, so the front and back of the house were exposed. We constantly had people stopping by to try to see our kids. We couldn't even let them play outside on the weekends, as people would take photos and post them on the Internet.

Our lives got more complicated with public appearances and other media that came along with it; but we realized we could never go back to our pre-public days, and we still needed to provide for our family.

We already couldn't develop our photos because of the security risks of the photos being taken and posted online or worse, sold. To this day, thousands of family pictures are filed away on the computer, waiting to be printed. People—and this is just fans of the show at this point—would come up to the bay window at the front of our house and take photos. We had to keep the blinds drawn at all times to try to regain pieces of our privacy.

In the fall of 2007, one specific eye-opening event occurred. Our family had an appearance on a local cable show. While we were waiting to go onstage, a man was in the waiting area who claimed he was somebody's driver. He put our kids on his lap and took pictures of them, and nobody could do anything to get rid of him. I kept mentioning my discomfort as politely as possible, but whenever he was asked to leave, he kept reappearing. I felt powerless and completely creeped out; so from then on, we traveled with security at my insistence and had the total support of the network. There was no going back.

Besides, it was essential for safety. With eight small kids in airports and just two of us, what were Jon and I going to do if someone snatched one from us? We had seven others to keep an eye on. Security assistance meant we could just focus on our kids and let someone else watch people's intentions.

It always thrills me when my kids have the privilege of flying.

❄ ❄ ❄

Overzealous attention was bad enough, but when those actions turned into vandalism, it became ugly. Our mailbox was destroyed several times, our house was egged, among other things. We were already confined inside with the blinds drawn the majority of the time, and I felt horrible because this was no life for any kid. They need to be free to run outside and play. So I constantly felt torn between keeping them safe and allowing them a normal childhood. They just wanted to ride their bikes on the driveway. Seriously, was that too much to ask?

They just wanted to ride their bikes on the driveway.

At the request of the network, a security review was completed on our house and it highlighted areas where security needed to be improved. Unfortunately, neighborhood building codes prevented us from making the necessary adjustments, so we needed to look into a more secure home location.

It took awhile for us to find the right house. When we finally found it, we had a moving plan in place set for the end of November, right before the holidays. It couldn't come soon enough for us.

That summer when we were on a vacation in North Carolina, Jon and I said to each other, "Let's just not go home. Let's stay here." If only! We dreaded going home.

When we were home, I would wake up every single morning and the first thing I would think about was, "Where can we go? How can we get away from here? Where can we go where people aren't staring in our windows?" I felt there was never anywhere we could go to get away from the prying eyes. Twenty-four hours a day, seven days a week, cars were parked along the street. People were watching us at every moment. I would look out my window and see somebody with a camera pointed into my bedroom window taking a picture. We were constantly reminded that we couldn't keep our own children safe. As a mom, I was horrified. I felt like I wasn't doing my job.

I started viewing everyone as our enemies. I'm sure most of them didn't mean any harm; they were just curious. Each person driving by probably thought he or she was the only one who drove by our house. What they didn't realize is that "just one person" five hundred times a day gets excessive day after day after day after day. We felt bad for our neighbors because we brought so much chaos to the neighborhood. Besides the fans (and vandals), tabloids started calling the neighbors, and reporters started knocking on their doors in addition to our own.

We needed to get out of there fast.

The last straw came unexpectedly one October morning. As I headed out to work on a new book with my editor, I jumped in our white minivan and as I started to back out, I realized it had two flat tires. Annoying, but I could just take the Big Blue Bus instead. When I saw that the bus had two flats as well, I noted that this was not an accident. After closer inspection, I saw large gashes in the tires and realized that someone with a knife had walked up our driveway and deliberately slashed them in the middle of the night.

I ran back in the house and yelled, "Jon, we need to move now!"

I had heard there was a lot of anger toward me on the Internet, but why would someone do this? I not only felt violated—and upset, since we now had to pay for four new tires—but I no longer felt we could keep our kids safe. The crime happened right underneath Mady and Cara's room. What was to stop this person, who was obviously armed with a weapon on my driveway, from taking it further? He could have just as easily smashed the windows, entered the house, hurt our children, and set the whole house on fire.

My mind was not lacking in coming up with horrible scenarios. Since people were coming up and knocking on our door, what was to stop them from acting out my worst nightmare—abducting one of my kids? One adult in charge of eight kids was not good odds to be able to stop somebody. We needed to move immediately.

As we put the plan in motion to move that fall weekend, I realized that our circumstances had drastically changed. We moved in as a happy little family—okay, maybe not so little, but certainly naive—and moved out older and wiser.

We moved in with a U-Haul truck, but moved out with a security company and unmarked trucks so no one would know our new address—or that we were moving at all!

We moved in not thinking twice about giving out our email, cell, address, and other personal contact info, but moved out only sharing our post office box address with the outside world.

We moved in grateful and excited if someone dropped off a package on our doorstep, but moved out having been instructed by our security team not to open any unexpected items.

You can imagine that we did start to question our chosen profession with the increasing security issues. But any parent with a dangerous job has to make the same choices. Think about cops, firefighters, and military personnel. I'm not comparing skills, only the risks involved in any chosen career. Every job has its ups and downs, and we still saw this job as having far more benefits than risks: We were able to work at home with our kids, paychecks were coming in to pay our bills, our kids were able to travel and have experiences they wouldn't have had otherwise.

What it really came down to, though, was that privacy infringement and security risks—which were the negatives of this job—would continue even if we stopped the show immediately, but without the positives.

So once again, we found ourselves in unusual territory. Our differences did not stop with having two sets of multiples. Everything about our lives felt weird and abnormal at that point. I still struggled to make life as normal as possible, but frankly, we never were normal—from the way we went about things to the places we went, the times of day, and the days of the week that we had to go anywhere.

Thankfully, the house we were moving into would let our kids have as much of a "normal" childhood as possible. They wouldn't be locked indoors with the blinds closed anymore. Thank God!

When we went as a family to see the new house for the first time, Leah gasped and said, "Thank you, Mommy!" as we pulled up to the driveway. Seeing a four-year-old that appreciative is so rewarding. Those kinds of reactions are why I can keep going. When we opened the door, all eight kids began screaming and took off running in various directions throughout the house.

They love that house so much. In our old house in Elizabethtown, day in and day out, no one could get away from each other—no rest, no quiet, no privacy. Kids were in every nook and cranny—with no personal space except their own beds. Some of my first memories of the new house include seeing Aaden sitting on the couch, reading a book alone, without someone bothering him. I had never seen this happen in the old house. It was just too small. While it looked big on TV and served its purpose well, we really didn't have enough room for everyone, and the kids didn't have their own space.

Even though people now know where our new house is, it provides space and security. If our kids can't always go out in the real world safely, at least they can run around protected in their own house and yard. And I've now learned the ropes of what to do to keep them out of harm's way. Looking back, I see that I did not always handle situations well, and I probably seemed like a safety nut. (Okay, let's face it, I'm still a safety nut!) But no matter what the situation is, as mothers, our first priority is our kids' safety, health, and well-being.

I also have to remind myself that while I've taken every safety precaution possible, their safety is still not 100 percent guaranteed. I learned quickly when I was pregnant with the six that ultimately I have to trust God. I can't control the outcome, but I do pray constantly for God's protection. When they're on the school bus, I pray for them. When I'm out of town, I pray for them. When they're driving in the car with other people or in someone else's care, I pray for them.

And now that I can let go and trust God for my kids' safety, I can look back fondly on those past few years we lived at that house with the red door on Andrew Avenue. I learned quite a bit there, and those lessons are the foundation we're building our life on now.

I've learned how to better control my drama and how to handle things differently. I don't let every little thing bother me anymore. When we first moved into that house, if someone spilled a glass of milk, it would send me over the edge and ruin my day. Now I don't even blink. I hand the mess-maker a paper towel and move on.

Overall my perspective on what is really important has changed. And I'd like to think these changes are for the better and will continue to help me deal with whatever comes my way. I'd also like to think that these changes set a positive example for my kids when they see me navigating the unexpected twists and turns of life that come my way daily.

Letter to Joel

✻

Dear Joel,

My sweet, quiet boy, you were born last but certainly not least!

At fourteen weeks, at my routine ultrasound appointment, I learned that you were a boy—making Daddy and I both very happy because you were the first, and quite possibly as far as we knew at that time, our only boy. It wasn't until weeks later that we learned we were having three boys—and three girls too! However, I remember that day well. I pondered all day and the rest of the week the fact that I was carrying my first baby boy as one of my six babies! It was such a novel idea after having your big sisters.

You spent your twenty-nine weeks and five days on the top right side of my belly. You were positioned on top of Collin. At the time, he didn't seem to mind and neither did you. Directly across from you was Leah. You and Leah had the best real estate in my opinion. Early on, I discovered that I was most comfortable lying on my right side, so that meant that although you had space originally, in reality you were pretty squooshed! Sorry, Joely!

It all turned out okay because you, my last baby ever, were born on May 10, 2004, at 7:53 in the morning. You were nothing but pure gorgeousness when I first laid eyes on you, just eight hours after your birth. In fact, I recall being very startled at the sight of you because I had never seen a baby that looked so very much like his daddy before.

In the days to come, your favorite NICU nurse, Heidi, would write messages on the tape that kept your feeding tube in place. This tape was attached to the area around your mouth, so it was as if you were actually saying, "I love you, Mommy and Daddy." That really melted my heart because I loved you so much! I love you that much, and more, today.

As I've watched you grow into yourself, I am glad that I "won" the battle of your name. I really had to plead with Daddy for a "Joel" and now I can't imagine calling you anything else! You're Joel, Joely, and sometimes even Joely Man! The latter reminds me of your stuffed animal "Doggy Man" that you named all by yourself when you were two. The funny thing is, Doggy Man isn't very manly at all. The poor little gray doggy (I think he's a Scottie dog, maybe?) came wearing a predominantly pink and purple girly sweater. Poor guy, but you two became fast friends and you love him just the same.

Speaking of men, you are becoming one right before my eyes! You have already shown your ability to protect me and your sisters, and that makes me very proud. You and your brothers are the only three men in my life now, and I appreciate your stepping up and helping out within your five-year-old capabilities.

I sometimes become impatient with you being so easygoing, laid-back, and good-natured. I am sorry that my rush-rush personality sometimes doesn't see the beauty in stopping to smell the roses as you often tend to do. Please forgive me, Joely, as I work on this issue.

I have many memories of trips taken as a family when you won the best traveler award—specifically, on the long flights to

Hawaii and Wyoming (so much fun, remember?). I was astonished at how quiet and composed you remained. You are typically happy, helpful, and sweet no matter the circumstance. I admire these traits in you.

When I think of you, I can't help but picture your amazing smile and even more so your giggle that is infectious! When you start laughing, everyone around laughs with you, literally. It is refreshing to have you in our family. You are the perfect final piece in our puzzle!

In the recent months, as our family puzzle has changed and you and I have begun to accept this fact and deal with it, there is one thing I need you to know: My love for you will never ever change. This love I have for you will be constant, steady, and unconditional—always—until my last minute of my last day.

I am sorry that I do not have the skills to father you, but I am committed to properly mothering you to the best of my ability. I want you to persevere throughout life, Joel. I want you to work hard and never give up. Anything worth doing is worth working very hard for. I want you to develop a burning dedication and commitment to those things you deem worthy of your time. These are admirable qualities that will take you far in life!

I desire deeply for you a rewarding career, successful marriage, and a life filled with happiness, love, and lots of your laughter! I pray that you grow to love God and follow him always. Allow his guidance in your life first and foremost. Life will be difficult, and in the same token, enjoyable. Hang on, Joel, and finish the race strong. I will run alongside you, cheering you on—louder than anyone because I'm your biggest fan.

Thank you, Joel, for teaching me to slow down and enjoy life.

I've enjoyed seeing it through your eyes, and those of your brothers and sisters. I didn't pick you, nor you me, but even if we had had the opportunity, we could never have done such a perfect job!

I love you, buddy, forever and always, no matter what,

Mommy

13

LETTERS OF LEGACY

My parents taught me some invaluable lessons — lessons I'm trying to pass on to my own kids. Dad instilled in me a strong work ethic and financial responsibility. I remember him spreading out bills on the dining room table and inviting us kids into his process. He always put us in charge of adding stamps and an address label to each envelope. I have tried to follow in his footsteps by always paying my bills on time, working hard, and being as financially responsible as possible. Soon I'll have eight stamp and address label applicators of my own.

Mom, on the other hand, was a constant, steady presence in our lives. She had a home-cooked dinner ready each and every evening and always did her best to keep up with five rambunctious kids!

My grandparents, too, taught me so much, especially about the value of family. They knew I had always wanted to be a nurse, and they watched me work as hard as I could to pay for school. Using babysitting money, I paid for the first year myself but realized I didn't have enough to continue. Even though they didn't have much money to spare, my grandparents paid for my final two years of college. I continued working diligently throughout my schooling not only for myself but for my grandparents as well because they invested in me. When I graduated, Grandpa sent me a letter: "You're going to make a real fine nurse. We're really proud of you, honey."

I still have that letter.

As Grandma and Grandpa got older, I started to collect the other letters they sent. Grandma always sent me cards of encouragement, and Grandpa would take pictures, develop them, and then send them in the mail with a note written in his curly handwriting. They never failed to bring a smile to my face through their letters full of love, encouragement, and belief in me as a person.

Dear Katie,

Sure was good to hear from you. Keep on hanging in! We love you and know you're going to be a real beautiful nurse.

Grandma has the kitchen all messed up by baking pies. She says there's a small grape pie for us two. The others go to our pastors.

When you are here we can talk about your need for whatever you need prior to your operation [tonsillectomy].

We love you,
G'pa & G'ma

Dear Katie,

We really appreciate your letters. You are more important in our lives than you seem to think. We have so many happy memories of you and your siblings. We treasure them all. You were an important part of family during all those growing up years.

Grandpa

Thank you for the love letter! We love you too.

G'ma

Dear Katie,
Sure was good to hear from you. Keep on hanging in! We love you and know you're going to be a real beautiful nurse.

Grandma has the kitchen all messed up by baking pies. She says there's a small Grape pie for us two. The others go to our pastors.

When you are here we can talk about your need for whatever you need prior to your operation.

We Love You
Gpa & Grma

This is one of many sentimental letters from my grandpa.
I cherish each one.

As you have already noticed, I'm partial to love letters. Maybe it's because letters are a lasting form of communication. Or maybe it's because you know the writer spent quite a bit of time thinking about the recipient. All I know is how much letters have meant to me throughout my life.

One of my favorite chapters in the Bible was actually first written as a letter, but it is more commonly referred to as the "Love chapter." In fact, I got Hannah, Leah, and Alexis' middle names from this chapter.

> *Love is patient, love is kind. It does not envy, it does not boast, it is not proud. It is not rude, it is not self-seeking, it is not easily angered, it keeps no record of wrongs. Love does not delight in evil but rejoices with the truth. It always protects, always trusts, always hopes, always perseveres. Love never fails ... And now these three remain: faith, hope and love. But the greatest of these is love.*
>
> *1 Corinthians 13:4– 13*

❀ ❀ ❀

Grandpa struggled with congestive heart failure following a heart attack while I was pregnant with the six. His weakened heart took him from me in the end, but I know his love for me remains.

After Grandpa died in June 2005, we knew it wouldn't be long for Grandma. They had been married sixty-five years, and they loved each other fiercely. Theirs was an amazing and rare love story right up until the very end, when Grandma cried, "I just want to go be with Grandpa."

One Saturday evening in September 2006, my sister-in-law came over to babysit the little kids, so the girls, Jon, and I could go to Lancaster General Hospital to visit Grandma. On our way we made a wrong turn—and then another one. We drove around Lancaster for about an hour.

Frustrated from what it took to get there, we rushed in to find out visiting hours had just ended. Determined to visit regardless, we walked in to find Grandma pulling out her IV. She looked up, and with recognition on her face, she said, "I haven't seen you and Jon in years!" We didn't have the heart to tell her we just saw her the previous week. As the nurse was putting her IV back in, Grandma remarked that she had never been so embarrassed in her life. Then in the next breath, she turned to her nurse: "Did I do that?"

It hurt to see Grandma like that.

"How are you, Cara and Mady?" I was so happy she recognized the girls! They would have been heartbroken if she didn't. I doubt she remembered we had six others, as she didn't say her famous line: "You always wanted a little brother and he broke into six little pieces."

I held her hand once the nurse left, the IV back in place. I wanted our deep loving relationship to go on forever, but as I sat there with her, I realized it couldn't. "Grandma, I love you," I said, "and even though I'll miss you, it's okay if you want to go home to be with Grandpa. I don't want to be selfish anymore."

"I always liked you the best!" Grandma replied.

This was not the Grandma I knew. She would have never shown favoritism. It was so hard not to see her act like herself.

I looked into her eyes and I could still remember my dear Grandma and all the years of pure bliss that she and Grandpa worked hard to create in their grandkids' lives. The love she and Grandpa had for everyone and anyone—even those who appeared to be unlovable— was powerful.

I suppose I knew the day would come when we would be without them, but I had always pushed it out of my thoughts. As we each gave Grandma a kiss goodbye, I had a sinking feeling in my stomach.

A week later, I was lying awake in bed in the middle of the night; I kept feeling guilty about not going back right away to visit Grandma again. My sister had told me I needed to visit her soon since she wasn't doing well. I had so many logistical reasons for not going back over to the retirement home after she was discharged from the hospital, but the excuses didn't seem to matter anymore. I had a distinct feeling that I had lost my chance.

When I woke up the next morning, I brushed that feeling off and headed to work. As I was finishing putting my first patient on the dialysis machine and getting ready for the second, the phone rang—which is not an uncommon occurrence, but everyone was too busy to pick it up. About a minute later, the phone started ringing again. I had a feeling it was Jon, so I watched my co-worker Cindy closely as she answered it. As she turned to me, I knew it wasn't good. When I took the phone, Jon told me Grandma had died, and I sobbed, wishing I had been able to hug her goodbye one last time. She had just turned eighty-nine.

❈ ❈ ❈

After our family's first special aired on TV, when we would visit Grandma in the retirement home, her friends would ask, "Oh, Ruth, are these your grandkids?" She was always so proud. She was a great Great-Grandma!

While Grandma and Grandpa got to meet all their great-grandkids, I'm sad they didn't get to know them better. I'm grateful for the memories I have of Grandma singing with our one-year-olds at our six-seater table, captivating them with her Girl Scout songs and the accompanying motions.

"Mom, tell us the story about Grandma and Grandpa," Alexis loves to ask. "Show us the letter from Grandpa!" I'm always glad she asks, because I'm trying to share with my kids stories of my grandparents' legacy.

Grandma and Grandpa taught me empathy, care, concern, and love. They were busy people, but they always stopped to pay attention to the small things. They loved watching birds, and I can picture my grandma saying, "Art, did you see that cardinal? Wasn't it exquisite?"

Grandma and Grandpa were my examples of unconditional love. They loved people—all people. And everyone was welcome at their house anytime for any length of time. They gave everything they had. Whoever met them, never forgot them. That's just the kind of people they were. They would receive hundreds of Christmas cards every year, and Grandma had baskets and baskets full: forget displaying them, there were way too many.

My best childhood memories were the times we spent at their house. We would have New Year's Eve parties and stay up all night long. We also had tea parties, using Grandma's fine china for tea, and pretending raisins were caviar. We'd put on all of Grandma's costume jewelry and bright red lipstick—and then, of course, we'd kiss the duke (aka Grandpa). We'd cook up a storm and destroy Grandma's kitchen for the millionth time, while she'd cheerfully say, "I'll get it," as she cleaned it up. Even the hour ride to their house was memorable.

Grandma and Grandpa picked us up in their pickup truck, and we would ride in the back on the wood storage boxes Grandpa had made. We'd tumble around in the back and then open the sliding window in the back of the cab. Grandma would talk to us or tell us to get drinks out of the cooler or sing the whole way to keep us busy.

Grandma was a fabulous cook, but when she asked us what we wanted for dinner, we would always choose "plastic turkey and plastic mashed potatoes," which is what Grandma called TV dinners. She didn't mind—she would let us have them anyway.

While they had a whole house full of bedrooms, we slept on the floor in sleeping bags in their bedroom. We'd listen to them snore in their well-rehearsed chorus. In the mornings, Grandpa got up early and made us a big breakfast in his clanky cast iron skillets and brought Grandma coffee. She stayed up so late, so she always had a hard time waking up in the morning. We would jump on her, and she would never get angry or annoyed. (Wish I could say the same ...)

I can still picture Grandpa sitting peacefully on a bench in the utility room, watching TV and carving Bible verses into his locally famous plaques with a pocketknife. He kept a peanut can full of bubble gum in the cupboard. He would chew the gum when he took his false teeth out at night, and he would always share his gum with us—especially the grape-flavored pieces, which were our favorite.

Grandma always had a purse full of candy and was known as the "candy lady" at church. All the kids found her after the service to choose a piece of candy.

Looking back, they taught me what really matters: family, memories, tradition. I couldn't have asked for better grandparents. Soon after we moved into the house on Andrew Avenue, we placed the birdfeeder Grandpa had made for us outside our dining room windows. Almost immediately, two doves moved in. With the loss of Grandma and Grandpa always on our minds, coupled with the fact that they were avid bird watchers, it seemed only fitting to name the doves Grandma and Grandpa. Each evening as we ate dinner, without fail "Grandma and Grandpa" were there to pay us a visit. It was as if they were watching over us, and strangely, this was very comforting to all of us.

Grandma and Grandpa doves on our back deck
(near Grandpa's bird feeder).

❄ ❄ ❄

Because Grandma and Grandpa's letters meant so much to me, I started writing letters to my own kids. Every Saturday before I left for work I used to write notes to Mady and Cara. Something as brief as:

Dear Cara,

I hope you have fun today. Please be a big help to Daddy. I hope you enjoy dinner tonight— Nana Janet Roast with mashed potatoes and gravy, your favorite! I'll see you tomorrow morning when you wake up. I love you!

Love, Mommy

At first I just thought it was a nice way for them to wake up, but later on I realized they came to look forward to and expect those little notes each weekend. I only recently discovered that they saved them. I found stacks of notes in the drawers underneath their beds!

In addition to the everyday notes, each Valentine's Day I write a love letter to each child. While in the day-to-day routine I have to be tough, Valentine's Day is a special time for me to remind them in various ways how much I love them. In fact, all day on Valentine's Day, I ask the kids what Valentine's Day means, and they respond, "Looove!"

The tooth-fairy notes came soon after that. Jon and I were sleeping when Mady presented us with her first tooth. On Mady's note I wrote:

Dear Mady,

I would like to introduce myself: I am Miss Tooth Fairy! I flew from far away to collect your tooth— and thank you, by the way. I am working on a necklace. Enjoy your surprise! See you next time a tooth falls out! (But please wait until it's warm outside, since I don't like flying in this chilly night weather!)

Byeeeeeeee, Miss Tooth Fairy

Oh, and one more thing: Brush your teeth. I don't like dirty rotted teeth! Thank you!

We left that first note with a $2 bill. (The dentist said the going rate in our area for the first tooth is $20. Not so much in our house!) We were so busy with the little kids when Mady and Cara started losing teeth, that at one point, Mady lost a tooth and the tooth fairy didn't come for five days. She was heartbroken. We left her a note from the tooth fairy that read, "I'm sorry, I broke my left wing. I could only fly in circles." We had to come up with something because we had been so forgetful.

I couldn't keep track of only Mady and Cara's teeth, so I can't imagine how hard it will be with six of them. When they start losing teeth, I'm going to have to prepare preprinted notes and have them all folded and ready. Even the tooth fairy needs some organization and efficiency.

Cara lost her first tooth and proudly showed me.

When Mady and Cara started first grade, I wrote napkin notes in their lunches almost every day. I remember how much little notes meant to me during lunchtime, and I want them to feel the same way I did. My mom used to write her notes in red ink with the same curly handwriting as my grandpa and she always signed them "1–4–3" (I love you).

In addition to the lunchbox notes, there is always a note on the dry erase board by the sink that I change periodically. For Thanksgiving it read, "I'm so thankful for each one of my eight perfectly amazing kids." For Christmas it read, "You're the

Love notes sent from someone who loves us! Aaden and Alexis open their cards I left at their places at the table—standard mail delivery protocol in our house!

eight best Christmas presents I could ask for." For Valentine's Day it read, "My heart belongs to each of you."

❊ ❊ ❊

The best surprise is that the kids now leave notes for me.

Mady received a plate to decorate for Christmas. Recently, when I was traveling, she decided to decorate it and then so sweetly chose to give it to me. When I got home, she left the Christmas plate in my room with two Post-It notes stuck to it. One note said, "Dear Mommy, I decided to decorate and give my plate to you, because you're the most important person to me." The second one read, "Do not touch unless you're Mommy."

I love the plate, but you know I will never ever remove the Post-It notes.

All those nights when I sat completely exhausted at my laptop and could barely see the computer screen through my blurry eyes, I continued to journal and make notes of our daily, seemingly mundane lives. Even though I thought I'd remember what happened each day, it has gone by so quickly that many of the memories have all but faded. With each journal entry, each note, each event and conversation recorded, my kids will have a permanent reminder of my love for them during these early years. But this legacy is far from complete: I'll continue writing my kids love notes because I just want them to know how much I love them.

ACKNOWLEDGMENTS

To J.M. for everything—enjoy your new baby (aka Squooshy)!

To S. & G.N. for your unwavering support and for including us as part of your family.

To J.A. & J.M. for your undying lifelong friendship.

To C. & A.T. for answering my SOS calls over the years.

To J.N. for stepping in whenever needed and taking over perfectly.

To A.S., K.C., J.S., and B.P. for your work on this book.

To T.G., J.B. & R.D. for making me look good, and to N.P. and M.L. for an amazing cover.

Photo Album

    In the process of writing this book, I was looking for photos to include. Because I had never seen many of them before, I spent hours reliving those years in our home on Andrew Avenue. I hope you will enjoy these pictures as well.

Our first day of ski school in Utah. It took two hours and lots of adults to dress all of the kids. I was so happy they had the privilege of learning to ski.

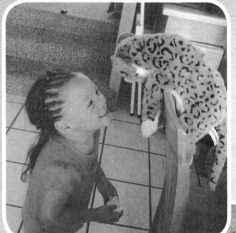

At the beach in North Carolina, Alexis greets "Dusty." I have no idea where she came up with the name Dusty, but he is her buddy for sure!

All six kids giving one another "rabbit ears." It's moments like these that I can catch glimpses of the future ... when they are all teenagers doing goofy stuff to each other (heaven help me!).

This is one of my favorite pictures of Aaden ever ... from the snack in the corner of the mouth to the folded down ear.

Cara in her own design. She always came up with the most creative paper hats and masks.

Diving into our Easter baskets before church. There was no room for everyone to go and spread out their contents, so they ended up sitting on the floor around the dining room table ... sneaking jelly beans (organic of course) at any chance.

Life's a beach, isn't it?

On a rainy beach day, Leah, Alexis, and Hannah made the pantry into a fun game—jump out and scare Mommy!

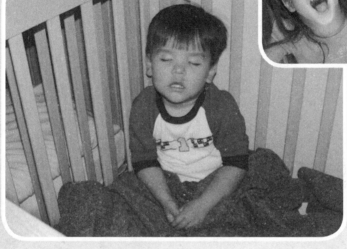

Collin clearly had an issue with "lying down and going to sleep"— so he sat up and went to sleep during this naptime!

Collin enjoying a winter wonderland right outside our door!

Mady did her hair up in chopsticks and was
proud to show off her Asian heritage.

Mady got a karaoke machine for Christmas and sang all day— and all night!

Hannah and Leah had fallen asleep at the top of the stairs near their bedroom … It was time to put a gate at the top for safety!

Fun at our neighbor Laura's pool. They graciously allowed our eight kids to descend upon their backyard pool each and every Wednesday morning one summer.

Alexis stopping for a water break at her third birthday party.

Out to dinner and spending time with Hannah and Leah.

As we packed for a winter trip, Hannah decided
to wear Mommy's shoes for a day.

Hannah, Cara, Collin, and Joel on the "party bus"
as the kids always called any bus (other than ours).

Collin is lifting a "BIG" pumpkin … or trying. He called them "balls." This was taken on the first episode of our show.

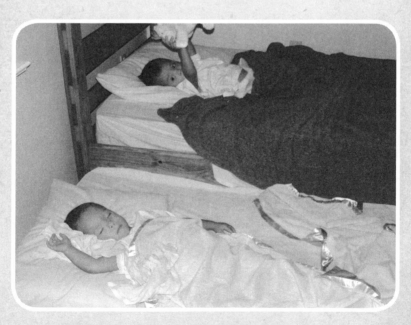

First night in our new big boy beds. What a milestone. I sadly watched as our last cribs ever were replaced with beds. Aaden is sleeping, while Joel is playing—typical!

Hannah, Collin, Leah, Alexis, Joel, and Aaden
showing off dress-up and favorite toys.

Mady and Cara's sixth birthday at American Girl Place in New York City.
What a huge treat for my big girls (and for Mommy)!

The first summer at Andrew Avenue, our friend Carla
introduced us to the amazing world of butterfly hatching!
We took turns releasing them. Each child got to release two butterflies.
Here it's Cara's turn and Mady and Alexis watch.

Hannah having a counter
conversation with Mommy.

All eight kids in five square feet! The kids
were thrilled to be in a store picking out
equipment for our infamous rainy campout.

Miss Beverly always had a way of not only folding, but also
entertaining at the same time. I think the kids were in "boats" here.

In loving memory of Nana Janet.

Enjoy these recipes from Kate's new cookbook,
Love Is in the Mix. *Coming soon!*

Nana Janet's Roast

2 Tbsp butter

2 Tbsp olive oil

4 lb bone in chuck roast

1 large onion,
  sliced thin

1 tsp coarse salt

Water

¾ cup flour

Rinse defrosted roast and pat dry. Place oil and butter in large saucepan with lid. Melt over medium high heat and then place roast in pan and salt with half tsp salt. Place sliced onions on top of roast. Sear roast on one side until medium brown. Flip roast and salt with remaining ½ tsp salt. Sear second side until brown. Add 1 cup water (about ½–3/4 inch of water in bottom of pan), reduce heat to medium and cover. Cook until most of the water dissipates (about 10–14 min). Flip roast, add another cup of water, cover, and cook again until water dissipates. Repeat steps for 2 1/2–3 hours. Do not allow water to completely disappear so roast won't burn.

During last water addition, cook roast for 5 minutes and then remove roast from pan. Turn liquid up to boil and add flour slowly while stirring to create gravy. Serve with mashed potatoes and a green vegetable.

This is a most tender and delicious roast beef. It's especially wonderful in mid winter when it's very cold outside. I remember asking Nana Janet for this recipe. She said she'd have to show me—she showed me alright! We got busy talking and we burned it, so she said with a laugh, "I showed you what NOT to do!" So don't walk away from this one!

Mommy Applesauce

15 apples (I like to use Golden Delicious)

½ cup water

1 cup white sugar

2 tsp cinnamon

Core, peel, and thinly slice (about ½ inch thick) apples. Combine all ingredients in slow cooker. Cover and cook on low for 5 hours. Once applesauce has cooled, use a hand mixer to make smooth applesauce.

*Variation: Omit sugar to make Baby Applesauce. Freeze in small container for baby—as one of his first foods!

My kids rave over Mommy Applesauce! There is nothing as easy or as rewarding as this crock-pot applesauce recipe. I freeze it in containers to bring out and thaw (and reheat!) for dinner.

An added bonus? As it cooks, it makes the house smell better than the best apple cinnamon candle you can buy!

Thomas Hummus

3 cans (16 oz. each) chick-peas

18 Tbsp lemon juice (or juice from 6 lemons)

4 garlic cloves, minced

3/4 cup tahini paste

6 Tbsp olive oil

1-1/2 tsp salt

Drain chick-peas, reserving ¼ cup liquid. Mince the garlic. Puree chick-peas with liquid, garlic, lemon juice, garlic, tahini, oil, and salt until very smooth.

Serve with pita bread or pita chips (see below).

Can be stored up to 4 days in the fridge.

Pita Chips

Slice pita bread into triangles and arrange on a cookie sheet. Spray with olive oil and sprinkle lightly with salt. Bake at 450 degrees for 7–9 minutes until pita slices are golden brown and crunchy.

Store in a Ziploc bag for 2–3 days.

Our kids call hummus "Thomas," thinking it's named after Collin Thomas. They have been eating it since they were very young and often yell, "More Thomas please!" This is a great lunch or healthy snack, and I often serve it with raw veggies.

Memorable Pizza Meatballs

2 lbs ground beef

2 cups seasoned bread
crumbs

1 cup milk

½ cup onion, finely chopped

2 tsp pepper

1 block (8 oz)
mozzarella cheese

1/3 cup flour

¼ cup oil

50 oz pizza sauce (our
favorite is Don Pepino)

Combine first 6 ingredients just
until mixed and shape into meatballs. Cut mozzarella cheese into
cubes and put one into the center
of each meatball, covering the cheese completely with meat. Roll lightly in
flour. Cook meatballs in oil over medium heat until browned (about 3–4
minutes each side) and then drain. Add pizza sauce and bring to boil. Turn
down heat, cover and simmer for 20 minutes or until meatballs are cooked
through. Makes approx. 32–40 golf-ball size meatballs.

Serve over pasta, rice, in buns, or as an appetizer.

*We first tried these during that first year with six crying babies. It seems an
unlikely hit, but it has made its way to our table many times—and has become
a definite favorite. I serve them with fries and steamed broccoli. It can also be
served on rolls and becomes pizza without the crust. This is a great recipe to serve
half tonight and freeze half for a quick future dinner!*

Grandma's No-Bake Chocolate Cookies

2 cups sugar

½ cup milk

½ tsp salt

2 heaping tsp cocoa

2 Tbsp vanilla

½ cup peanut butter

2-1/2 cups oatmeal

Bring sugar, milk, salt, and cocoa to a boil and continue for 1-1/2 min. Remove from heat and add vanilla, peanut butter, and oatmeal. Line countertop with wax paper and use a teaspoon to drop mixture onto paper. Allow cookies to cool and harden. Makes approx. 3 dozen cookies.

This is one cookie recipe that is safe for kids as young as mine to help. I mix the ingredients together and then transfer dough to smaller bowls and provide a spoon and a sheet of wax paper to each child. They enjoy spooning their own cookies onto their own wax paper. These cookies are also a great source of fiber and are fun to make together!

Eight Little Faces

A Mom's Journey

Kate Gosselin

Just in time for Mother's Day, this gift book features photos from Jon and Kate's family album, along with words from Kate on a variety of topics any mom can relate to including patience, encouragement, gratitude and guidance. Kate's favorite Scripture verses accompany the text.

Follow the lives of the entire Gosselin clan in words and pictures.

Available in stores and online!